W9-ACI-486

ECE/TRADE/282

ECONOMIC COMMISSION FOR EUROPE
Geneva

BUSINESS ADVISORY, COUNSELLING AND INFORMATION SERVICES

UNITED NATIONS
New York and Geneva 2002

ECE/TRADE/282

UNITED NATIONS PUBLICATION
Sales No. E.01.II.E.25
ISBN 92-1-116792-2
ISSN 1020-8119

List of Abbreviations

BAS	Business Advisory Services Programme (Multi-Donor Programme based at EBRD)
BCC	Business Communication Centre
BC–NET	Business Cooperation Network (EU)
BDA	Business Development Agency
BEST	Business Environment Simplification Task Force
BIC	Business and Innovation Centre
BIN	Business Information Network
BMGDB	Moravian Guarantee and Development Bank (Czech Republic)
BSI	Business Support Institution
BSC	Business Support Centres
BSS	Business Support Services
CEI	Central European Initiative
CIS	Commonwealth of Independent States
CIT	country in transition
CNC EBN	Czech National Committee of EBN
EBAN	European Business Angel Network
EBN	European Business and Innovation Centre Network
EBRD	European Bank for Restructuring and Development
EEDC	Employment and Economic Development Centre (Finland)
EIC	Euro Info Centre
FFE	Federation of Finnish Enterprises
FGB	Finnish Guarantee Board
GDP	gross domestic product
IAPMEI	Institute for SME and Investment Support (Portugal)
KOSGEB	Small and Medium Industry Development Organization (Turkey)
LEDU	Local Enterprise Development Unit in Northern Ireland
MIT	Ministry of Industry and Trade (Czech Republic)
MLSA	Ministry of Labour and Social Affairs (Czech Republic)
MRD	Ministry for Regional Development (Czech Republic)
NASA	National Aeronautics and Space Administration (USA)
NBDA	National Business Development Association (Czech Republic)
NDG	National Discussion Group (Czech Republic)
NGO	non-governmental organization
OECD	Organisation for Economic Co-operation and Development
OSDBU	Office of Small and Disadvantaged Business Utilization (NASA)
PT	Employers' Confederation in the Service Industries of Finland
QQI	Quality, Quantity and Institutionalization as a measure of success applied by OSDBU
RAIC	Regional Advisory and Information Centre
SBA	Small Business Administration
SBDC	Small Business Development Centre
SBS	Small Business Service
SME	small and medium-sized enterprises
SMEA	Small and Medium-Sized Entrepreneurs' Association (Croatia)
TAM	TurnAround Management (Multi-Donor Programme based at EBRD)
TMG	TurnAround Management Group at EBRD, running TAM and BAS programmes
TT	Finnish Industry and Employers
UNCTAD	United Nations Conference on Trade and Development
UNDP	United Nations Development Programme
UNECE	United Nations Economic Commission for Europe
UNIDO	United Nations Industrial Development Organization
USAID	United States Agency for International Development
WASME	World Association for Small and Medium Enterprises
WP.8	UNECE Working Party on Industry and Enterprise Development

Foreword

This handbook is a result of the work of 120 experts in 15 UNECE member States as well as a dozen international organizations who have gone through an extensive consultation process of drafts and updates to collect and complement information regarding the current status of advisory and counselling services in the UNECE region.

The work is based on a recommendation of the UNECE Meeting of Experts on Best Practice in Business Advisory, Counselling and Information Services that was held in Geneva on 2 and 3 November 2000, where the delegates agreed that support services that improve the potential for SMEs and trade in services and effective competition in the international market remain a high priority in the UNECE region. Some barriers to the development of entrepreneurship and trade in services can be so fundamental that without their removal, there are practically no conditions for the development of entrepreneurship or services.

The goal of this handbook is to be a guide to the current state of the art in the UNECE region. The secretariat has reviewed and edited the contributions of member States and international organizations.

The results are now presented in this UNECE handbook. In part 4 "Conclusions and Recommendations" the conclusions and recommendations adopted by the UNECE Meeting of Experts are presented for consideration of the member States.

We hope that this handbook as the second publication in the UNECE series of Best Practice in Enterprise Development can help those dealing with the promotion of entrepreneurship, trade in services and the development of enterprises to gain further insight into the different concerns as well as successes that have been collected in the UNECE region regarding support services for entrepreneurship.

Brigita Schmögnerová
Executive Secretary
UNECE

Acknowledgements

The UNECE Secretariat wishes to thank you the following individuals and organizations for their valuable contributions to this book:

Albania: Mr. Idajet Ismailaj, Mr.Dhimitraq Marko, Mrs. Alxeta Veseli. *Austria*: Ms. Sylvia Hofinger. *Azerbaijan*: Mr. Ragib Guliyev. *Belarus*: Mr. Vladimir Gousev, Mr. Valeriy Skakun, H.E. Mr. Anatoly Skorbezh, Mr. Victor Tanaevsky. *Belgium*: Mr. Jean-Louis Duhaut, Ms. Anne Verbruggen. *Bosnia and Herzegovina*: Mr. Nedim Dzano, Mr. Muamer Peljto. *Bulgaria*: Mr. Vladimir Pavlov. *Croatia*: Mrs. Katarina Jagic, Mrs.Dragica Karaic, Ms. Ivana-Barbara Turkalj. *Czech Republic*: Mr. Pavel Komarek, Mr. Jan Martinek, Mrs.Marie Pavlu. *Finland*: Mr. Risto Suominen. *France*: Mr. Jean Vimal du Monteil, Mr. Thomas Viron. *Germany*: Mrs.Margit Mund, Mr. Hans-Jürgen Reichardt. *Hungary*: Mrs. Andrea Ambrovics. Mr. Laszlo Bus, Mrs. Marianna Pongorne Csakvari, Mrs. Anna Daniel, Mr. Gergely Gyula Kovacs, Mr. Laszlo Kallay, Mr. Gyorgy Lendvai, Mr. Tamas Lesko, Mr. Mihaly Plesoczki, Mr. Attila Szentagotai, Mr. Peter Szirmai, Mrs. Marta Takacsne-Toth. *Ireland*: Mr. Bob Keane. *Israel*: Mr. Yaakov Livshits. *Italy*: Mr. Mauro Castagno, Mrs. Simona Cigliano, Mrs. Nicoletta Marchiandi, Mr. Alberto de Paoli, Mr. Carlo Salvato, Mr. Carlos Talamas. Kazakhstan: Mr. Nurlan Alpiyev, Mr. Bektas Mukhamejanov, Mr. Bakytzhan Sagintayev. *Kyrgyzstan*: Mr. Tolon Toichubaev. *Latvia*: Ms. Astrida Burka, Ms. Lilija Stelpe. *Malta*: Mr. Ray Muscat.   *Poland*: Ms. Krystyna Gurbiel, Mr. Darius Kaluzny, Mr. Andrzej Kidyba, Ms. Maria Anna Knothe, Mr. Henryk Stasinski, Mr. Boguslaw Szweda, Mr. Krzysztof Wiktorowicz. *Republic of Moldova*: Mr. Viorel Berlinsky, Mrs. Elena Chislari. *Romania*: Mrs. Maria Grapini, Ms. Cornelia Rotaru. *Russian Federation*: Mrs. Irina Alexeeva, Ms. Elena Emelianova, Mr. Victor Ermakov, Mr. Vadim Grishin, Mr. Sergey Ilyushin, Mr. Alexandr Ioffe, Mr. Anatolij Kazakov, Mr. Serguei Khvan, Mr. Victor Lisin, Mrs. Zoya Molokova, Mr. Serguei Poliakov. Mr. Leonid Shevelev, Mrs. Nadezda Shmelkova. *Slovakia*: Mr. Jan Hudacky, Mrs. Katarina Kellenbergerova, Mr. Ivan Pezlar, Mrs. Darina Trojakova. *Slovenia*: Mrs. Stasa Baloh-Plahutnik, Ms. Viljenka Godina, Mr. Bozidar Marot, Ms. Alenka Marovt, Ms. Janja Podvrsnik, Mrs. Maja Tomanic-Vidovic. *Switzerland*: Mr. Martin Gollmer, Ms. Sonia Heptonstall, Ms. Joyce Jett, Ms. Elizabeth Kaczorowska. *The former Yugoslav Republic of Macedonia*: Mr. Blerim Zlatku. Georgia: Mr. Mevlud Tsiklauri. *Turkey*: Mr. M. Mutlu Oktem, Mr. Kadir Yazihan. *Ukraine*: Mrs. Olga Apatenko, Mrs. Tetyana Darydyants, Mr. Dmitro Derkach, Ms. Olena Kuchkova, Mr. Victor Mayorchenko, Mr. Vladimir Milovsky, Ms. Eleonora Nikolaichuk, Ms. Olena Osynska, Mr. Oleksandr Pokreshchuk, Mr. Sergii Tretiakov, Mrs. Lyudmila Yakovleva. *United Kingdom*: Mr. David Pirnie, Ms. Michele Shirlow. *United States of America*: Mr. William Cain, Mr. Edward Reinauer, Mr. Duane Shelton. *European Commission*: Ms. Martine Diss, Mr. Bruce Harris, Ms. Veronica White.

Organizations: United Nations Conference on Trade and Development (UNCTAD): Ms. Lorraine Ruffing. United Nations Industrial Development Organization (UNIDO): Ms. Elisabeth Merz, European Bank for Reconstruction and Development. TurnAround Management Group at EBRD: Mr. Chris Walker. International Cooperative Alliance (ICA): Ms. Gabriella Sozanski. Organisation for Economic Co-operation and Development (OECD): Mr. Jonathan Brooks. World Association for Small and Medium-Sized Enterprises (WASME): Mr. Ralph Thomas.

Background

The United Nations Economic Commission for Europe (UNECE) organized an Expert Meeting on Best Practice in Business Advisory, Counselling and Information Services at the Palais des Nations in Geneva, Switzerland, on 2 and 3 November 2000 within the framework of the Commission's Regional Advisory Services Programme as part of the programme of work of the UNECE Working Party on Industry and Enterprise Development (WP.8). The meeting was the third in a series.

The meeting aimed at exchanging experiences in the creation and operation of business support service institutions in UNECE member States, sharing information on successful business advisory, counselling and information centres, and determining conditions to ensure the sustainability of these institutions.

Nearly 150 senior policy makers and experts from 33 countries and 10 international organizations, including representatives of 42 non-governmental organizations, attended the meeting. In addition, the meeting was attended by representatives of the following international organizations: European Commission; United Nations Conference on Trade and Development (UNCTAD); United Nations Industrial Development Organization (UNIDO); European Bank for Reconstruction and Development (EBRD); International Cooperative Alliance (ICA); Organization for Economic Cooperation and Development (OECD); and World Association for Small & Medium Enterprises (WASME).

The Meeting was opened with an introductory statement made by Ms. Danuta Hübner, Executive Secretary of the UNECE. Ms. Staša Baloh-Plahutnik, Under-Secretary of State of the Ministry of Economic Affairs of Slovenia was elected Chairperson and Mr. Ragib Guliyev, Chairman of the State Committee on Antimonopoly Policy and Support for Entrepreneurship of Azerbaijan Co-hairman. Mr. Antal Szabo, Regional Adviser on Small and Medium Enterprises acted as the secretary and Mr. Mika Vepsäläinen, Enterprise Development Officer, as rapporteur of the Meeting. An ad hoc working group was set up to prepare conclusions and recommendations, which were adopted by the meeting. They are presented at the end of this publication.

For further information, please visit the UNECE website at www.unece.org/trade or contact the UNECE secretariat: e-mail:enterprise@unece.org or by telephone +41 22 9173197 or fax +41 22 9170178.

Contents

Contents continued

PART I
INTRODUCTION

The number of enterprises in the non-primary private sector has grown to over 19 million in the European Economic Area and Switzerland, providing employment for more than 110 million people. The majority of these enterprises are classified as small and medium-sized enterprises (SMEs). The 5 million SMEs in the countries of the Central European Initiative (CEI) have more than 25 million employees. The United States has over 22 million small businesses that employ 53% of the private workforce and account for over half of the national economic output.

SMEs both in advanced market economies and in transition economies find it harder than larger businesses to find and use the information and advice they need. The burden of regulation is particularly heavy for them. To address this situation additional work needs to be done in a number of areas. Among the many solutions proposed, business advisory, counselling and information services seem to be the most effective means of assisting entrepreneurs in improving the competitiveness of small businesses.

Many countries attach great importance to the preparedness of entrepreneurs to acquire knowledge and to be able to use the results of innovation results and new information. The UNECE, too, sets a high value on the development of SMEs both in advanced and in transition and emerging market economies. In this work, we have recognized that Governments can and must help in creating an enabling environment for SMEs so that they can more easily cope with the ever-increasing challenges.

In the countries in transition and emerging market economies, the most significant problems for SMEs include the transition to the culture of entrepreneurship, the acquisition of business and management skills, and technical awareness of the product and service quality demanded by market driven economies. Only when these attributes are in place, and there is a supportive and regulated economic environment, can one anticipate the sustainability of SMEs sector.

The SME sector needs to improve entrepreneurial ability and access to knowledge for business planning, marketing and compliance are critical to these needs. When clear strategies and viable supporting business plans are in place, access to finance is less of a problem, though until the commercial banking sector recognizes and respects the needs of SMEs, there remains a need for interim measures which are accessible to, and affordable by, the SMEs.

SMEs facing these and similar problems find business advisory, counselling and information services one of the most effective means of overcoming some of these kinds of difficulties.

However, the services have to be valuable to entrepreneurs since, in the longer term, business advisory services have to be justifiably supported, or self-sustaining, as well.

Particularly in the case of an institute relying on public funding, there must be a strong and clear reason for existence. Therefore numerous qualitative and quantitative evaluations have to be made. Another issue is how the effectiveness of this service can be measured. It is very popular and easy, but not always accurate, to look at the number of start-ups and relate this to the business support service.

Another important aspect is that a public institute is in the position to give advice to a potential start-up in an independent, neutral and objective way. It can be that negative advice is perfectly good advice taking into account the feasibility of the total project.

In order to help establish a common approach, the European Union has prepared a definition of business services as a group of different activities, based on which standard modules can be developed and transparent services provided to clients.

Fig.1 Needs of Start-ups

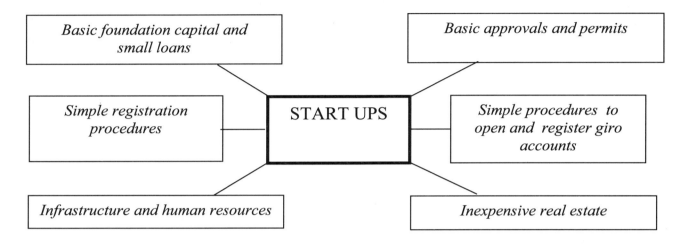

Fig. 2 Needs of operational SMEs

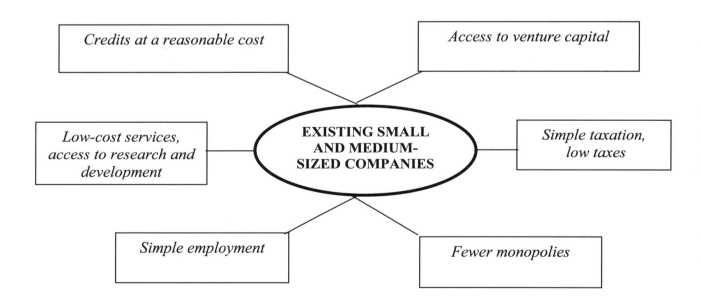

Source: "Voucher System for Consulting in Slovenia", paper prepared for the UNECE Expert Meeting by Mr. Bozidar Marot, Head of Financing and Marketing Division, Small Business Development Centre, Ministry for Small Business and Tourism, Ljubljana, Slovenia

Similarly, the European Bank for Reconstruction and Development (EBRD) has developed a standard approach to assistance in these areas. Many UNECE member States have developed their own systems over the years.

These models – both the standard ones and the models developed to suit a particular situation in a certain country – are described below as the current best practice in business advisory, counselling and information services available in the UNECE member States.

CHAPTER 1.
BUSINESS SERVICE INSTITUTIONS FOR THE DEVELOPMENT OF SMES

The significance of business support services in the creation of successful enterprises, and economic growth of SMEs is well acknowledged. It is generally argued that SMEs have certain deficiencies because of intangible assets that drive their competitiveness in marketing, management of production, innovation and information technology.

Among the support institutions, business advisory, counselling and information centres have proved to be particularly effective instruments for assisting entrepreneurs in starting new businesses, strengthening existing enterprises and helping their survival during the start-up period. More than 500 business advisory and information centres and business support agencies exist throughout the UNECE region, among them 274 Euro Info Centres (EICs) established with the assistance of the European Commission. In central and eastern European countries, 43 EICs are in function. In the Baltic States, there are two EICs and one correspondence centre. In the USA over 1,000 business support institutions have been established by Federal agencies and the 50 states.

There are more then 160 Business and Innovation Centres in Europe including 11 centres in central and eastern European countries. All these centres are members of European Business Network (EBN), which was founded in 1984 with assistance of the European Commission.

The EBRD established a Business Advisory Service Programme for support of SMEs in the Baltic States in 1995 and in north-west Russia (St. Petersburg) in 1999. The programme also covers Croatia, Bosnia and Herzegovina and Slovenia and a feasibility study on the potential for business advisory programmes in Kazakhstan and Uzbekistan has been carried out.

Business services help the SME sector realize its potential contribution to innovation and growth. According to the experience of the European Commission, some of the most dynamic SMEs use business services to perform functions that cannot be undertaken in-house. A greater use of these services by a wider range of SMEs should be encouraged to help them cope with the pressure of internationalization.

Governments of advanced market economies orient their policies and programmes towards fostering entrepreneurship and they are mounting specialized services and action plans to address these needs. In the European Union, the Business Environment Simplification Task Force (BEST) is charged with simplifying the business environment for small firms in Europe. In the United States, the Small Business Administration (SBA), established in 1953, has long been the principal instrument for the design and implementation of policies for small business. Similarly, Portugal administers SME policies and programmes through the Institute for SME and Investment Support (IAPMEI), and Turkey through the Small and Medium Industry Development Organization (KOSGEB). Enterprise Ireland was created in 1998 to assist small, growth-oriented companies and streamline support structures and the United Kingdom has set up the Small Business Service (SBS) to act as a voice for small firms and to improve the quality of business support.

Guidelines on Best Practice in Business Advisory, Counselling and Information Services allows the reader to get an overview of the policies and activities of central, regional and local Governments, SME-support institutions, research and development organizations both in economies in transition and advanced market economies dealing with these issues in their respective countries. These shared experiences, and the contacts that have provided the information will help officials and experts in other countries to intensify international cooperation.

The aim of the *Guidelines* is to describe:

➢ experiences gained in creating and operating business support service institutions in UNECE member States;
➢ how to create and operate successful business advisory, counselling and information services;
➢ how to ensure the sustainability of such institutions.

CHAPTER 2.
DEFINITION AND CLASSIFICATION OF "BUSINESS SERVICES"

SMEs are to be assisted not just because they are small, but because of their capability to be efficient, innovative and their ability to compete both in the national market and internationally. To assist them, professional technical and consultative services need to be provided through support systems and infrastructure.

The European Union defines Business Services as a group of different activities. The different functional characteristics of enterprises explain the number of these activities. Business Services include highly advanced consultancy services, professional services, marketing services, labour intensive services and security services, as well as human resources development and innovation policy focused on technology oriented SMEs.

According to the Common Policy Framework of the European Commission "The Contribution of Business Services to Industrial Performance" (COM 1998 534, Brussels, 1998), the business service classification consists of 26 activities in 8 sub- sectors. The activities are:
➢ Computer and related services
  ▪ hardware consultancy
  ▪ software consultancy
  ▪ data processing
  ▪ data base services
➢ Professional services
  ▪ legal activities
  ▪ accounting
  ▪ tax consultancy
  ▪ management consulting
➢ Marketing services
  ▪ market research
  ▪ advertising
➢ Technical services
  ▪ architectural activities
  ▪ engineering activities
  ▪ technical testing and analysis
➢ Renting and leasing services
  ▪ renting of transport and construction equipment
  ▪ renting of office machinery incl. computers
➢ Labour recruitment and provision of personnel
➢ Operational services
  ▪ security activities
  ▪ industrial cleaning
➢ Other services
  ▪ secretarial assistance
  ▪ translation activities
  ▪ packaging activities
  ▪ fairs and exhibitions

The United Nations Conference on Trade and Development (UNCTAD) sees as one of the most important tasks in developing SMEs the creation of effective business development services which have the following core principles:

Demand-side orientation and adaptation to users' needs. It is extremely important to instigate a dialogue with SMEs, help them identify and evaluate their own needs. This will help them to strengthen their links with local service providers and other support institutions.

➢ **Focused, strategic and collective approach**. Some services can be extremely cost effective when provided to clusters of small businesses operating in close geographical proximity, and can provide unique opportunities for fostering or strengthening links between small enterprises themselves.

➢ **Subsidiarity**. Services must be brought as physically close to small-scale entrepreneurs as possible. Government institutions should make indirect use of local support structures. Where business development services are strategically important but not yet adapted to local needs, joint efforts by public and private institutions have proven to be effective responses. They are one-stop centres, sometimes specialized, where entrepreneurs have access to a whole set of services needed to develop their businesses.

➢ **Market oriented and businesslike**. More attention is now being paid to the possibility of increasing the participation of the private sector in offering SME services. The private sector includes trade or industry organizations, chamber of commerce, business associations, semi-public institutions, private consultants and non-Governmental organizations.

➢ **Cost recovery**. Business development services are expensive. If cost recovery is a policy imperative, some of the costs can be reduced by providing services to groups of similar businesses in the same sub-sector or located close to each other. In order to reach increasing levels of cost recovery, small businesses must improve profitability and productivity through their services, which makes them willing to pay higher prices to access additional services.

➢ **Cross-subsidization services and clients**. Marketing, technology, accounting and legal services have clearly proven their potential profitability or financial viability. Other services, such as access to information and training, are not as profitable because of "free-rider" effects or because the need is not clearly perceived. This means that the revenues earned by viable services may finance a number of complementary services which are less viable but which are believed to have a beneficial impact on participating enterprises or on the market as a whole.

➢ **Sustainability** is only assured when the service provisions have reached a status (by regulation, state or other long term budget provision, or commercial viability) when they can survive and develop without other external intervention. This requires that both the demand and the supply are monitored so that continuity of services is truly determined by real needs and delivery of services that truly and economically respond to those needs within the local market context. Experience in many countries shows that this may take longer than is often envisaged in the planning stages and is probably not achievable in a period of less than 10 years.

➢ **Monitoring, evaluation and performance indicators**. Monitoring should cover the relevance and timeliness of services delivered and should be linked to regular evaluation of the direct and measurable impact of Business Development Services on the enterprises in terms of changes in productivity, profitability, quality, sales and employment.

At the macro level, the most important constraints to SME development lie in:

➢ The degree to which real markets for goods and services exist in the regions;
➢ Business environment - the legislative and regulatory framework, the banking system and contract enforcement;

➢ The delegation of the provision of services to the lowest possible level as close to the enterprises as possible;

➢ Access to affordable financing in appropriate conditions.

At the micro level, the following requirements for business services institutions can be identified:

Deficiencies in the quality of support services

➢ Confusion between the objective of creating business service institutions or helping SMEs. The former objective takes a decade, the SMEs need help now.

➢ Mainly supply driven services, which are not responding to a needs assessment of the demand-side; business services institutions must be familiar with and adapt to their clients' needs.

➢ Collective approach: the value lies in the efficiency of serving a number of clients together rather than one-on-one.

➢ Cost reduction and sustainability: the high cost of business support services necessitates support or cost reduction, e.g. reducing cost by providing services to groups of similar businesses in the same sub-sector or located close to each other. In turn, cost reduction for small businesses implies that after using services they must improve their profitability and productivity, this is what makes them willing to pay higher prices to access additional services. In the long term, cost recovery is an element of the sustainability of business services.

➢ Cross-subsidization is a technique of using a differentiated fee scale to pay for those who need services but are less able to afford them (e.g. richer clients pay for services to poorer clients), or to pay for the provision of less profitable services by using revenues from services with higher profit potential (e.g. offering training and information services by using profits from marketing, technology, accounting and legal services).

➢ Monitoring and evaluation are necessary to assess the Business Support Institution's (BSI's) performance and to ensure their efficiency. Evaluation of BSIs is based on the following criteria: outreach, measured in number and diversity of clients; cost-effectiveness, measured in cost per person; impact, measured in employment creation, increase in survival rate of SMEs, and profits; and sustainability. Monitoring and evaluation should not be done by the BSIs. The responsibility must be delegated to an independent institution.

CHAPTER 3.
GENERALLY APPLIED MODELS OF BUSINESS SUPPORT INSTITUTIONS

Governments and international organizations can influence both the supply of and the demand for business services. They can promote intangible investments by the private sector in R&D, training and education and business organizations by supporting the supply of these services through a range of intermediary supply bodies. Business Centres operate in many different countries, under different names and labels, but all with the same goal of advancing the position of SMEs in today's fast growing economy.

Business Development Centres

Below, we shall give an overall description of the most common institutions available in a number of countries. Individual countries will describe their respective services and the features that are specific to the particular country in the following sections.

.

Azerbaijan

In Azerbaijan more than 40 regional Business Advisory Centres help to develop small and medium-sized businesses in the whole country.

Belarus

"Belbusinesscentre", the Belarus Support Centre advises potential entrepreneurs on how to start a business. It gives market information and helps in drafting company documentation, including a business plan, and also gives advice on taxation, licensing and certification for small business owners.

Czech Republic

The Business Development Agency was established as a Government non-profit organization. It then established a network of 22 Regional Advisory and Information Centres and 5 Business Innovation Centres throughout the country. The Regional Advisory and Information Centres are private firms and provide a range of basic services that focus on counselling, legal and tax advice, bookkeeping and assistance in completing bank loan applications. The Business and Information Centres offer a complete range of services focused on technology oriented SMEs, as well as industrial support services.

Israel

The Small Business Development Centres (SBDCs) in Israel operate as independent, self-sustaining "one-stop shops" which respond to the needs of small business owners and entrepreneurs planning new businesses. Most of the SBDCs operate locally, usually in cooperation with the economic development agencies of local authorities. The goal of the centres is to aid entrepreneurs and SME owners in establishing, managing and expanding their business or in preventing their collapse. The SBDCs disseminate information in various realms, such as initial assessment of business concepts, information on permits and licenses required for establishing a business, investors and necessary contacts, and also referral to additional information sources. They counsel in preparing business plans, financial management, pricing, tax planning and the management of sales and marketing. The

centres organize courses and workshops specially suited to small and medium business owners and new entrepreneurs.

Poland

The mission of the Polish regional development foundations is to support the development of SMEs and, in doing so, to support the local economy and to promote the region both domestically and internationally. To create an environment conducive to enterprise development, the foundation offers advisory and consulting services, training as well as guarantees for loans. They develop networks of SME support organizations in the country.

Russian Federation

There are a range of services assisting SME development, such as the Federal Fund for Support of Small Entrepreneurship, the Russian Association for the Development of Small Sized Enterprises, and the Russian Agency for Development of Small and Medium-sized Business. In 1992, the Government created the Russian Agency for Development of Small and Medium Business Support. The Agency has in turn created a regional network of agencies, covering more than 50 regions in Russia. The agencies offer services for examining investment projects; expert financial advice; auditing and accounting. They provide information about business partners, about the region's business climate, about legislation, taxation, accounting rules, and reporting. They also help prepare contracts and documentation, give legal support in negotiations and registration and also organize courses and seminars on how to run a business in Russia.

Turkey

The Small and Medium Industry Development Organization (KOSGEB) is a non-profit semi-autonomous organization in Turkey. It provides technical, management and consulting services to small and medium-sized industries. Development centres, one of which is the Turkish Foundation for Small and Medium Business, carry out the actual functions and activities. It has created a network of 1,500 registered members, 17 support associations and two branches to provide support to its members and other SMEs.

United States of America

In the United States the Small Business Administration (SBA) was created as an independent agency of the Federal Government to aid, counsel, assist and protect the interests of small business concerns. SBA administers the Small Business Development Centres (SBDC). It provides management assistance to current and prospective small business owners and offers one-stop assistance to small businesses by providing wide variety of information and guidance in central and easily accessible branch locations. It delivers up-to-date counselling, training and technical assistance in all aspects of small business management. The SBDCs also make special efforts to reach minority members of socially and economically disadvantaged groups, veterans, women, and disabled persons.

The SBDCs are sponsored by lead organizations. These organizations coordinate programme services offered to small businesses through a network of sub-centres and satellite locations. Sub-centres are located at colleges and universities, community colleges and vocational schools, chambers of commerce and economic development corporations. Each centre has a director, staff members, volunteers and part-time personnel. SBCDs also use paid consultants, consulting engineers and testing laboratories from the private sector to help clients who need specialized expertise.

Business Information Centres in the USA are working under the Small Business Administration and provide a one-stop location where current and future small business owners can receive assistance and advice.

Business and Innovation Centres (BICs)

United Kingdom

The Small Business Service (SBS) is an executive agency of the Department of Trade and Industry in the United Kingdom. It helps small businesses realize their potential; acts as a strong voice for small firms; encourages the central and local Government and the European Union to "think small first"; and improves the competitiveness of small firms, especially by stimulating innovation.

Besides from the SBS, operated by the Government, SMEs can get help from many advisory services. For example, Business Support Services (BSS) excel in business development consultancy and aid companies achieve growth in marketing activities and increase their conversion rate from prospect to sale. Business Challenge Ltd. was created in 1991 to provide services for the small and medium-sized companies that were seeking cost-effective assistance and help in running their operations. It disseminates information about, for example, taxation, liquidations, Government assistance, as well as cash flow calculations, skill shortages and quality systems

Germany

Business information and consulting services in Germany are primarily performed by chambers of industry and commerce, as, stipulated by the law, membership is compulsory for all commercial companies. The chambers offer services free of charge. For instance, they advise firms on training courses and assist companies in acquiring public contracts and supply them with specific information about national and EU tenders.

Business Angels

Business angel networks are a very special form of Business Services. They are set up to provide means of introduction between investors (business angels) and small and medium-sized enterprises. Business angels invest in the companies, provide finance and expertise and also bring business skills to the enterprises. While the majority of business angel networks are publicly funded, some business angel networks work on a commercial basis or are sponsored by banks, venture capital funds or industry associations.

There is a great variety of business angel networks operating in the United States and in Europe. A tool for stimulating the creation of new enterprises and thus employment growth in Europe, such networks are also one of the priorities of the European Commission and several national business angel networks are partly financed by the European Regional Development Fund. National business angel networks started appearing in the United Kingdom in 1991. In the Netherlands, they have been operating since 1995 and in Finland since 1996. The European Business Angel Network (EBAN) was established a good year ago. It has two member categories: full members and associated members. The membership of the association is expanding, with new members from, for example, Switzerland and Israel.

One-Stop Shops

Business service institutions can act as "one-stop shops" for support and assistance. They can offer complex services and follow a project through right from the beginning till the very end. They can solve problems and provide answers to questions in short periods of time.

Generally one-stop shops have a real office but there are examples of virtual, Internet-based operations, too. A good example of the latter form is the Russian Virtual Office for Small and Medium-Sized Business, which has over 15,000 users. Another "office" that only operates on the Internet is the Lavanttal Innovation Centre in Wolfsberg (Austria), which connects companies, customers, suppliers, partners, as well as the operating management of the virtual office, with one another through the Internet.

It is common knowledge that the Internet infrastructure plays a crucial role in the development of business services. The Euro Info Centre Conference that was held in 1998 showed that, already then, over 43% of SMEs used the Internet and the figure has grown dramatically; primarily, as a result of e-mail communications, while enterprises seem less interested in putting information on their own websites. To improve the use of the Internet and to encourage network development among enterprises, some Euro Info Centres also provide web page design services.

In the framework of other business support networks than EICs, the European Union has created the "Dialogue with Business" service as a one-stop Internet shop for businesses and the "Cordis" programme as part of the European Commission's Innovation Programme.

"Dialogue" helps companies to do business in the European Market, gives advice on how to certify a business plan, helps search for business partners in the EU and informs about bidding for public contracts. The BC-NET (Business Cooperation Network) is an extensive network of correspondents who promote the concept of SMEs, and the "Bureau de Rapprochement des Entreprises" is a network of business counsellors, who assist SMEs with well-defined services in their search for cross-border cooperation.

The "Cordis" programme is the Research and Development Information Service of the European Commission. Designed to assist enterprises and, in particular, SMEs through the critical stages of technology transfer and innovation, it offers a wide range of services that keep entrepreneurs up-to-date on R&D and innovation activities in the European Union.

It operates the Network of Innovation Relay Centres (IRC), which, since their creation in 1995, have become a leading European network for the promotion of technology partnerships and transfer between SMEs. Today, there are 68 Relay Centres in the European Union, Iceland, Norway, Switzerland, Israel, Cyprus and 10 central and eastern European countries: Bulgaria, Czech Republic, Estonia, Hungary, Latvia, Lithuania, Poland, Romania, Slovakia and Slovenia. IRCs cooperate with other local agents and organizations such as universities, research institutes and industrial centres, which can call on IRC services to help transfer their results to industry. Each centre has business and technology specialists who possess thorough knowledge of the technological and economic profile of the companies and regions the centre serves.

A top priority for the IRC Network is to continually extend its contact base and strengthen the links between companies in all participating countries. To achieve this goal, the network has developed a portfolio of information services that responds to the specific needs of the IRC client companies in each region. The IRC Internet Site is a virtual meeting point for the members of the network and their partners. The site is divided into a public and private area. In the public area are the directory with lists of IRC members and their partner organizations, as well as hyperlinks to their respective web sites, and publications and success stories on recent technology transfer projects. The private area is a forum where IRC members can do business.

The Internet is more and more widely the communications tool and advisory service. Chambers of industry and commerce in Germany have established a national network for SMEs. They offer advice on how to use the Internet, how to set up online shops and how to create home pages, electronic payment systems etc. In Finland, SMEs' access to the Internet has grown rapidly over the past years. Two thirds of SMEs use the Internet. The most common use is still e-mail, followed by information searches. Recently, the use of the Internet for banking services has increased significantly. More than half of the clients of the Regional Advisory and Information Centre, Presov (Slovakia) use the Internet in their firms

World Wide Web and Internet Services

The advent of the World Wide Web has substantially changed the provision of business development services. For instance, the SBA in the United States has funded a virtual SBDC. The State Department sponsors a similar activity with a cyber business incubator to provide business support services in Ukraine as part of the American programme to support private sector development in the transition economies. Furthermore, private companies are increasingly providing free services for SMEs on their websites. Some companies provide these as a form of advertising to attract small businesses as customers, and some rent space on the site to other advertisers. Some sites are created by non-profit organizations, while some sites are purely a public service of altruistic individuals. Thanks to the Internet, much of this information is available to people worldwide.

CHAPTER 4.
INTERNATIONAL ORGANIZATIONS

International organizations play a vital role in SME development. Organizations attempting to engage in provision of services often fail to reach a critical mass. Therefore, they are best at facilitating and helping through providing public goods such as training, subsidizing production of training materials, measuring the impact of service, etc.

European Committee for Business Support Services (CESCE)

Founded in 1969, CESCE is an association of organizations, involved with the provision of business support to SMEs.

Its aim is to promote and broaden the activities of the affiliated organizations:
➢ By offering the member organizations a platform for the mutual exchange of knowledge and experience.

- By stimulating cooperation between the affiliated organizations, with a view to realise joint projects at a European level.
- By offering financial encouragement to the membership to internationalize their activities.

In this way CESCE is a European platform for the exchange of knowledge and experience. It is also a European network of organizations, offering business support to SMEs.

To achieve its goals, CESCE
- arranges workshops and experience groups, in which consultants, counsellors and trainers of CESCE members can participate.
- issues a newsletter to member organizations.
- functions as an information centre providing members with publications of fellow members that might be of interest.
- organizes congresses and symposia on subjects of interest to affiliated organizations.
- promotes joint actions for the implementation of projects and activities at a European level.
- offers subsidies to the partners to internationalize their activities.

Activities of the member organizations essentially consist of support, information, consultancy and counselling, as well as training and education to (future) entrepreneurs.

The target groups of the member organizations include (future) entrepreneurs and enterprises in the small and medium-sized enterprise sector.

European Business and Innovation Centre Network (EBN)

The European Business & Innovation Centres Network (EBN), an international non-profit seeking association, was created by the BICs, the European Community and a group of industrialists in 1984, to coordinate networking activities. By January 2000, EBN had over 200 organizations, including 160 BICs in 21 European countries and associated organizations from across the continent and further afield (Turkey, China, United States, South America).

EBN is now the leading network gathering BICs and similar organizations in Europe. It has become a reference point when talking about innovation, entrepreneurship, SMEs and regional economic development, in the EU as well as in partner countries.

The Association's task is to "promote inside and outside the European Union the development of Business & Innovation Centres".

More precisely, EBN's mission is to:
- Meet members' needs and requests for services
- Provide services and support members in their search for excellence
- Organize access to know-how and added-value information, and to share expertise and methodologies
- Strengthen member identity and competitiveness through monitoring the quality of the network and the EC-BIC label
- Support the positioning of the BICs and members as instruments recognized by policy-makers

The geographical priorities of EBN's action are the European Union and future member States. Partner countries of the EU are also involved.

Euro Info Centre Network (EIC)

One of the objectives of the European Union's enterprise policy is to help enterprises through better information services. To this end, Euro Info Centres (EICs) have been established in 37 European and Mediterranean countries, including the accession countries in central Europe and Cyprus, Malta and Turkey. These centres act as an interface between European institutions and local businesses as a European Commission network.

EICs act as a link between the European Commission and European enterprises. They use host structures, such as chambers of commerce, public services, professional associations, banks and services. EICs are established on a joint-financing principle, with the Commission providing only 10 per cent of the costs to run a centre. EIC staff must be well informed about EU legislation on SMEs, financing opportunities, activities and programmes. In turn, SMEs can use EICs to provide feedback to the Commission on problems and consequences of certain policies so that the Commission can adapt EU legislation.

Euro Info Centres inform enterprises on all Community policies, activities and programmes; assist enterprises in their efforts to expand and to internationalize; advise enterprises; and provide feedback information to the Commission on concerns and interests of enterprises, and on the impact of Community programmes and legislation. They organize seminars and meetings, publish and distribute news bulletins and guides and many centres run a website. As part of the EIC network in Austria, Finland and Greece, for instance, associated members make their specialized skills available to Euro Info Centres

The EICs help SMEs to transpose the various European regulations into concrete action and to search for partners. They advise SMEs on their participation in European programmes and projects and monitor the procedures to be followed by businesses that deal with European institutions. Some EICs have their own regional offices and run national networks.

The European Commission has set up a permanent evaluation of the performance of the network. The EIC Network is the only EU network that is evaluated on a regular basis and centres can be closed because of unsatisfactory performance.

The main success of the network lies in the fact that it is a physical network, not a virtual one. Different studies on SMEs indicate that only half of small companies have a PC in their offices, fifty per cent of SMEs do not use the Internet for research of business opportunities and many rely simply on e-mail. Therefore, physical proximity is absolutely necessary as well as an understanding of the specific needs in a particular community. The EIC Network is a real network because the info centres are linked. EICs offer indirect advantages, such as Internet and a conferencing system, working groups, training and exchange of experience.

It is important to avoid duplication of effort by the various business services support networks. The EIC Network has a mandate from the Commission to establish only one network under which different members offer specialized services and coordinate their work. The EIC staff are currently working closely with the Organisation for Economic Co-operation and Development (OECD).

Examples of the Euro Info Network

United Kingdom: Northern Ireland

Euro Info Centre, Ledu House is the lead agency for local economic development in Northern Ireland. It helps businesses that normally employ fewer than 50 people in the manufacturing and tradable services sectors.

Correspondence Centres outside the European Union

Correspondence Centres have been established in Israel, Latvia, Lithuania, Slovenia, Switzerland and Turkey. One of their purposes is to provide companies with services related to the European Union. For instance, the Euro Info Centre Switzerland, as one of the Correspondence Centres, gives information and advice, organizes seminars and courses for SMEs, diffuses EU legislation, sells publications and helps SMEs to look for business partners within the EU Member States.

Poland

The Euro Info Centre Warsaw acted as one of the two Europartneriat National Counsellors for Poland, making it possible for some 500 Polish companies to take part in the biggest European cooperation forum for SMEs. The centre also prepares foreign market analyses to help Polish companies to establish fruitful business contacts.

Romania

The Chamber of Commerce and Industry of Romania hosts a Euro Info Correspondence Centre to inform SMEs about the financial support offered by the European Union. It helps SMEs complete the documentation necessary for grant applications. Working together with managers of small enterprises, the Centre helps in the completion of feasibility studies and business plans, which are of utmost importance for a grant-winning project. The Euro Info Centres also help entrepreneurs find business partners.

EBRD Multi-Donor TurnAround Management and Business Advisory Services Programmes

The TurnAround Management Group (TMG) objective, agreed with all the Donors, is *'to assist enterprises to transform themselves so as to compete and survive in market economies.'* Both the TurnAround Management (TAM) and the Business Advisory Services (BAS) Programmes follow this objective, though by different routes, depending on circumstances. Both programmes work directly with the beneficiary enterprises, TAM is fully funded, though the enterprises must ensure significant contributions of senior management time, and must respond to the advice given, otherwise the projects are terminated and the funding is recycled to new projects. BAS, on the other hand, operates as a 'demonstration' project using local

consultants and requires a contribution to the costs, which operates on a sliding scale as the demonstration effect is shown.

Begun in 1993 as a trilateral Programme on behalf of EU PHARE, UNDP and EBRD, as of mid 2001, the TAM Programme has completed over 800 enterprise projects in 24 countries, while BAS has completed over 1,500 projects in 7 countries, but predominantly in the Baltic States. Ex-post and independent impact assessments have delivered an 80%+ rate of 'satisfactory or better' ratings for the enterprise transition in completed projects.

In delivering TAM or BAS assistance an early critique is made of the technical complexity of each potential beneficiary enterprise. For the more complex industries and commercial sectors the TurnAround Management Programme works directly with enterprises and provides 'industry specific' advisors [N.B. not consultants] to help the enterprises to understand the needs and opportunities of the national and international marketplace for their services and commodities and to make the necessary adjustments to management, marketing, design, quality and production, etc. so as to be competitive.

The BAS Programme adds a different dimension to the enterprise support sector and develops both the culture of using external consultants for precisely scoped business support in areas such as quality, accounting and stock control systems, local market research, etc. but also works on the assumption that there is a local consultancy resource of a quality that is able to deliver the services at an acceptable standard. Thus BAS facilitates the use of consultants and develops and improves the local consultancy capacity. In the event that a service is required which local consultants cannot provide, then a foreign consultant is introduced. However, they work with a local consultancy so that knowledge is transferred. To date more than 82% of projects are provided by local consultancy capacity.

An independent management group (the TurnAround Management Group) manages and delivers both the Programmes. Based in offices within EBRD, the TMG is established and governed by the TAM Rules and Regulations, which are approved by all Donors and authorized by the EBRD Executive Committee. A half-yearly supervisory board meeting guides the TMG and requires them to report all aspects of the Programme to the Donor community. TMG is self-financing and operates within the EBRD on a 'not-for-profit' basis on behalf of the donors who, since 1993, have entrusted € 56 million to the BAS and the Turn Around Management Programmes. The main donors have been the EU PHARE and Tacis Programmes, plus the Nordic Council of Ministers, the Russian Privatization Centre, the United Nations Development Programme (UNDP), and a wide range of bilateral donors, particularly Japan and the United Kingdom.

Eligible BAS enterprises are privatized with 10 – 250 employees. There is no turnover criterion. Eligible TAM enterprises tend to be larger, with a upper limit of around 1,000 employees, though the usual size is half that number.

United Nations Development Programme

The UNDP has produced the United Nations Inter-Agency Resource Guide on Small Enterprise Development (SED) to provide UNDP country offices and counterparts with a guide to the key services, tools and methodologies offered by those United Nations agencies on their small enterprise development (SED) activities.

These guidelines provide a common vehicle through which participating United Nations agencies can jointly advocate good practices in SED based on their shared experience with what works and what is sustainable. The Guide makes the link between the lessons learned and the tools available to apply those lessons optimally.

The Guide describes the enabling environment for the development of small enterprises and defines "good practices" summarizes the key findings of donors and practitioners in this regard, followed by a presentation of good practices for the specific services profiled. The services are grouped into seven categories as follows:

➢ *Enabling Environment and Policy Services*
- Provision of policy advisors
- National seminars promoting regulatory reform
- Governance issues

➢ *Training*
- Leadership and management training for entrepreneurs
- Financial and accounting training
- Computer and MIS training
- Business education (strategic planning, marketing, etc.)
- Economic policy and business development seminars
- Seminars in technical and cost strategies in bidding
- Training in institution building for business associations
- Training in industrial project preparation and appraisal
- Training in technology transfer negotiations
- Training in feasibility analysis methodologies

➢ *Business Advisory Services*
- Product enhancement (e.g., technical, packaging)
- Market development coaching
- Business planning and investment advice
- Quality management

➢ *Market Development and Trade*
- Trade management services for productivity
- Strategies to promote non-traditional exports
- Legal environment for exporters
- Customs management issues
- Export-oriented product marketing

> *Information*
> - Electronic commerce
> - Finding markets through the Internet
> - Information management systems
> - Business opportunities in business technology
> *Business Linkages*
> - Strengthening professional and trade organizations
> - building clusters and linkages among clusters
> - Vertical and horizontal linkages
> - Joint venture and sub-contracting options
> - Development and management of incubators
> *Technology Acquisition and Development*
> - Appropriate business technologies
> - Diagnostic analysis of production processes

The following criteria were used by the agencies to decide whether a service should be included in this *Guide*:

> the service should be based on commonly accepted good practices in the delivery of business development services;
> the service should have been available for at least two years;
> the service should have been tested in at least three countries;
> an external evaluation should have been completed on the service;
> the service should have an identifiable manager within the agency.

The understanding of what constitutes "good practice" in the provision of BDS has changed rapidly in recent years, and continues to do so. This has been a result partly of intensive work carried out under the auspices of the Committee of Donor Agencies for SED, which has organized a number of events and publications on the theme. The Committee published Preliminary Guidelines on good practice in BDS in early 1998. These are available in English, French and Spanish. They are widely circulated and are available from the International Labour Office and elsewhere.

General Principles of Good Practice in Business Development Services (BDS)

> Role of the State - Responsibility should be delegated to the lowest possible level and to those that are closest to small enterprises. In the case of the State, this implies that its role should not be to provide BDS directly. Rather, it should create an economic environment conducive to SED in order to facilitate BDS. It could do this by focusing on core functions of the State (health, education, infrastructure, basic training, law and order, and information networks), and by addressing market failures and improving equity.
> Business-like and demand-led - BDS should be provided on a transactional basis; those accessing the services should be treated as discerning clients, not as pliant beneficiaries. In general, therefore, there should be charges for services at a level that is significant for the client.
> Closeness to clients - Needs assessments should be carried out by someone with small enterprise and BDS experience who is close to small enterprise managers in terms of language and culture.
> An explicit approach to sustainability - Donor interventions, since they are short-term, must incorporate a clear exit strategy from the beginning. There should be a clearly articulated picture of the desired long-term future.
> A clear, strategic focus - The intervention should be both specific and relevant to the development objective(s). The provider must be competent in the specific service provided, the client must demand the service, and appropriate networks should be established.
> Participation: building on ownership - If services are designed only on the basis of external analysis, the intervention may not

succeed. Important complexities in the local situation may be missed and there will be less local 'ownership'. Nonetheless, and given that owners of small enterprises may not be fully aware of their own needs, demand-led approach can be achieved in many ways, for example, by rapidly modifying an initial offer in the light of feedback gained.

➢ Enhancing outreach - Donor-funded BDS has tended to reach only the 'fortunate few', relative to the size of the total target group. There is an urgent need to increase outreach, which may include sub-sector approaches (whereby relatively small and focused inputs may have a considerable impact on a whole sub-sector). Sustainable interventions have the potential to replicate and grow as has been seen in the field of micro-finance.

➢ Tight performance measurement - Measuring performance in BDS provision poses a number of significant methodological challenges. Nonetheless, it is increasingly important that interventions be built around achievement of certain performance goals, tightly defined and measured. Lessons learned from this process must, similarly, be incorporated into the planning process for future interventions.

These general principles can be differentiated by the type of service (the firm level), and the way in which they are delivered (the intermediate level).

Basic Capacities of BDS Providers

How the service is provided is as important as the design of the service itself. Important aspects of the capacities of local providers are:

➢ Organizational capacity - a business-like vision and clear corporate culture; clear target client group.

➢ Managerial capacity - decentralised structure; high degree of autonomy from the State; costs controlled and sustainability enhanced.

➢ Financial capacity - fees charged for services; economies of scale; services provided to groups rather than individual clients; diversified sources of funding.

➢ Technical capacity - specialized production in areas of expertise; ability to meet changing consumer demands, through service development and innovation.

These considerations apply to all types of BDS providers but it is now clear the intermediate level must increasingly cover a group of providers that has been largely ignored to date: for-profit BDS providers in the private sector.

Emerging Trends in Providing Business Development Services

For-profit trainers have been found to have some very important characteristics. First, their provision of BDS is sustainable; up-grading it is likely to reach larger numbers of small enterprises in the years to come. Second, they are sustainable because their aspirations are similar to those of the small enterprises they serve. For example, many earn $100-200 per month, which is clearly substantially less than most donor-funded trainers. They are also more likely to be training in the local language and in ways that are accessible to the poorest whereas much donor-funded training requires at least some basic literacy skills.

While considerable research is planned or on-going in this area, existing insights point to the following, additional good practices:

➢ "Do no harm"- As interventions are planned, existing for-profit providers should be carefully surveyed to ensure that their capacities are strengthened where possible. At least, their (sustainable) provision of BDS should not be displaced by high-quality but highly-subsidized services.

- Work within the private sector - When responding to demand from for-profit providers for strengthening, it is best not to mix them with providers who have traditionally been donor-funded. Indeed, donor funds should be used ideally only to strengthen providers rather than to subsidize BDS provision.
- Develop the overall market for BDS - If small enterprises purchase BDS on a substantial scale without any donor intervention, needs will presumably be satisfied best by a fully developed market where numerous providers compete with each other and discerning small enterprise clients choose the services they need.
- Enhance demand - BDS markets in the private sector are generally far from perfect. In addition to enhancing supply, there is much to be done to stimulate and educate demand from small enterprises. Training vouchers and matching grants are two interventions in widespread use, but more innovation is clearly required in this area.

Clearly, the use of donor funds to subsidize service provision has great potential to distort markets. This has created a trend whereby donors increasingly fund facilitators rather than providers. Facilitators take on some or all of the following functions:

- Mapping and monitoring BDS markets (both supply and demand)
- Providing appropriate support to existing for-profit providers by training trainers
- Supporting the marketing of their services, promoting networks of providers, etc.
- Demonstrating innovative services that are commercially viable, followed by a withdrawal from (or privatization of) direct service provision once copy-cat providers have started up
- Supporting those copy-cat providers
- Engaging in advocacy with Governments, donors and others to achieve greater consistency and support for the existing BDS market

- Acting as a buffer between donors and the small enterprise sector, which clearly operates within a different culture and financial scale. Thus, facilitators are responsible for donor funds, impact monitoring, etc.

Assessing Supply of Services

As overall Government and donor resources are limited and as many past supply-driven Government and donor-led interventions for support to small enterprise development have shown limited efficiency and impact, the imperative is to build upon what already exists, rather than creating new providers of business development services. In particular, there is an increasing consensus among practitioners and donors that the focus should be on supporting service providers that are predominantly market-based and independent of Government structures.

As in the case for determining needs and demands, a survey of the available supply of professional business services within the community has to be undertaken concurrently with the analyses of demands. This is even more important as new service providers, subsidized through the use of vouchers and other means, should not be allowed to undercut existing local supply. The survey of available providers has to look objectively at capabilities, relevance and affordability of providers as well as ability to adapt to the changing needs of the small businesses and their environment. Much of the information needed for the supply-side analysis can be gathered from surveys and discussions with customers/businesses. However, identification of suppliers and interviews with these suppliers should also take place.

A source of capacity building that many times is neglected is the ability of businesses to learn from each other through informal exchanges. Partners, suppliers and even competitors are potentially good sources for advice and sharing of experiences. Indeed, recent studies indicate that formal business development services reach a very small proportion (less than 5%) of total small businesses. Supporting the establishment and strengthening of business associations and similar mechanisms for exchange and cooperation among businesses, should therefore also be considered as an important supplement to the provision of direct service providers.

The full United Nations Inter-Agency Resource Guide on Small Enterprise Development can be found at http://www.undp.org/edu/

CHAPTER 5.
BENEFITS OF BUSINESS SERVICES

Benefits in general

The range and supply of business services have grown rapidly owing largely to their dynamism. Business services are flexible to the new needs of customers, new services are easily developed to help clients cope with rapid technological development. The services help reduce costs, improve the quality of the products of the clients and improve access to knowledge, skills, expertise and new technology. Business services also increase the effectiveness of technological inputs since advanced services like IT-services allow a better use of existing technology.

Business services also generate employment. For example, in the European Union, business service sectors employ more then 11.5 million people, representing 8.5% of total employment.

Benefits for SMEs

Working continuously with a large number of SMEs, business services accumulate the best current practices in areas such as drafting business plans, carrying out feasibility studies and preparing formal papers.

Business services advise on sources of finance, grants and other support forms and also provide access to information, which will allow the actual client enterprises to concentrate on their core business.

PART II
FUNDAMENTALS

CHAPTER 6.
BEST PRACTICE IN BUSINESS SERVICES IN ADVANCED MARKET ECONOMIES

Six papers were presented on this topic. The speakers highlighted their experiences in Belgium, Finland, France, Germany, Italy, and the United Kingdom.

In their presentations the speakers identified the major characteristics of business advisory, counselling and information services in their countries in the following five areas:

- Structure of business advisory, counselling and information centres
- Financing of business advisory, counselling and information centres
- Goals and types of services
- Education for entrepreneurship
- Role of technology.

The structure of Business Service Institutions (BSIs) in advanced market economies depends on whether they are public service institutions, sponsored by the respective Ministry, such as in Belgium, Finland, France, Italy, and the United Kingdom or independent bodies, receiving no public funding, such as in Germany. Whatever the case, in many advanced market economies there are also private institutions promoting entrepreneurship. Membership in the public BSIs, usually chambers of industry and commerce, may be mandatory, as is the case in France, Germany, and Italy. In Italy, in particular, membership is extended to everyone, including craftsmen and businesses involved in agriculture as well as small business. In Belgium and Finland, membership is not mandatory, but services are offered to entrepreneurs such as tradesmen, artisans and managers of SMEs.

Financing of BSIs varies from being exclusively financed from corporate taxes and operations, as in France, to being financed by subscription fees without public funding, as in Germany. In either case, however, cross-subsidization is practised so that companies pay in line with their economic capabilities. For example, in the Chamber of Industry and Commerce in Stuttgart, Germany, 95 per cent of the fee is paid by 5 per cent of the companies, belonging to the chamber. Thus, big companies pay to support the chamber's activities, while small companies do not pay anything or pay a very small amount and have access to business support services.

The goal of BSIs is to provide services to SMEs, including start-up, established and growth businesses. In Germany, however, the chambers of industry and commerce provide services to all companies of whatever size, from the "mom-and-pop" store to the large multinational. In the United Kingdom, LEDU (Local Enterprise Development Unit in Northern Ireland), the major BSI, offers pre-start activities such as enterprise awareness training and television advertising campaign to encourage enterprise activities.

It is generally recognized that start-ups should get at least one free consultation. People with commercial/business backgrounds usually deliver services. They are tailored to a company's needs and stage of development, e.g. start-ups or established companies, which would require different services. Services vary, with training, advice, information, and technical assistance being more prominent than providing finance directly. Other services include one-stop-shop facilities, technological and innovation think-tanks, promotion tools for international trade, advice on public-sector contracts, electronic commerce, marketing management, financial management, internal and external feasibility study, adult education/training, etc.

The provision of business advisory, counselling and information services in the advanced market economies is based on the following principles:

➢ Subsidiarity, i.e. delegating the provision of services as close to the clients as possible; thus, their needs can be met in the most effective way;
➢ Close contact with entrepreneurs, including regular visits;
➢ Personalized service, which in Italy is based on the life cycle of an enterprise and includes an interview to identify a project and computerized tests to assess entrepreneurship and risk;
➢ Partnership with local, regional, national and European actors;
➢ Entrepreneurs' ability to voice their views through the BSIs and to influence local or national decisions.

All practitioners in business advisory, counselling and information services in advanced market economies underlined the crucial role of entrepreneurship education. According to Mr Risto Suominen from the Federation of Finnish Enterprises in Helsinki, investments made in education are often more efficient and effective than publicly financed contributions made for promoting entrepreneurship. As noted by Mr Jean Vimal Du Monteil, Development Director of the Chamber of Commerce and Industry in Grenoble, France, entrepreneurship education is more than just know-how, but it is also a system of values and beliefs. A significant component in adult training must be devoted to inserting a motivation, especially when working with unemployed people, as noted by Italian speaker Mr Carlos Talamas from the Milan Chamber of Commerce.

The role of information technology is widely recognized as a crucial component in SME development. The most common use of the Internet is, no doubt, e-mail, and after that the acquisition of information. In most countries, use of the Internet in business activities is still not very common, although it has been steadily increasing. The exception is Germany, where the chambers of industry and commerce have established a nationwide network to offer consulting services on electronic business issues and the Internet to SMEs. Common questions include: how to set up online shops, create home pages, electronic payment systems, Internet connectivity, and teleworking.

In all European advanced market economies, Euro Info Centres provide information, advice and training in all areas relevant to SMEs.

CHAPTER 7.
BEST PRACTICE IN BUSINESS SERVICES IN THE ACCESSION COUNTRIES AND OTHER COUNTRIES IN TRANSITION

Nineteen presentations were made on this topic. The speakers were from Azerbaijan, Belarus, Bulgaria, Croatia, Czech Republic, Hungary, Poland, Romania, Russian Federation, Slovakia, and Ukraine.

In the early years of transition, in many countries the activity of the Governments focused primarily on privatization and restructuring of large State enterprises, while SME supporting programmes were mainly initiated by international donors. By now the importance of SME national policy is clearly recognized both by Governments and entrepreneurs. As a result of the earlier neglect of SMEs, many countries, notably the countries in transition, still lack a coherent national policy, which constrains SME development.

Three components of national SME policy were most prominent in the presentations: the definition of SMEs, the business environment, and the tax system. In this regard, the following characteristics were highlighted:

➤ Different definitions of SMEs circulate in associated countries and countries in transition, with consistency with the EU definition of SMEs in the first wave of enlargement countries (associated countries) and less consistency in other countries in transition.

➤ The business environment presents obstacles to both SMEs and business services institutions. This is especially relevant for countries in transition, where the major preoccupation lies with improving the legal and regulatory framework for business support services. For example, in Ukraine, the registration and licensing processes for SMEs constitute serious obstacles to their development. Therefore, it can be concluded that associated countries and countries in transition are at different stages in the provision of business advisory, counselling and information services, with more sophisticated business support services being offered in the associated countries.

➤ In all countries, there is clearly a need for a tax system that promotes investment and reduces bureaucratic barriers which increase operational costs and decrease companies competitiveness. One of the main difficulties faced by SMEs in all countries, is an excessive tax burden. Even in the more advanced associated countries for example Poland, recent tax changes have not resulted in making the system simpler and more uniform.

There are essentially two types of service provided by BSIs:

➤ Basic services, called "introductory consultations" or "information and general advisory services," are usually provided free of charge. These include one-stop-shop services, which are service packages required by national or foreign entrepreneurs and offered under one roof. One-stop-shops are considered to be time efficient and to discourage corruption. The Romanian Chamber of Commerce and Industry has implemented a successful one-stop-shop, which assists beginners to start up their businesses.

➢ Specialist advisory services or consultancy services consist of specialist advice in a particular area, e.g. general management, marketing and sales, production management, human resource management, etc. There is a general agreement that they should be offered in exchange for a fee.

BSIs can be State organizations, regional authorities, public/private partnerships, subsidized private agencies and companies, etc. In the light of the varied BSI typology, BSIs can be divided into the following categories:
➢ Entities providing services to SMEs
➢ Entrepreneur organizations
➢ NGOs focused on SMEs
➢ Research institutes and academic units.

Entities, providing services to SMEs, are usually non-profit organizations, specializing in the provision of advisory, information and training services to SMEs or start-ups. They can be grouped as follows:
➢ Business Support Centres
➢ Business Information Centres
➢ Business Incubators
➢ Innovation and Technology Centres
➢ Research Centres/think-tanks
➢ Non-profit financial institutions
➢ Regional Development Agencies.

It must be kept in mind that the terminology differs from country to country. In addition to these institutions, Euro Info Centres constitute prominent actors in business advisory services in associated countries. Forty-nine EICs have been established in seven associated countries.

BSIs employ various implementation instruments for achieving their goals in SME promotion. Some of these tools include:

➢ Start-up subsidies to increase the level of capital investment;
➢ Subsidies for regional investment, credit and loan guarantee funds;
➢ Business financing through equity investment;

➢ Partial financing of SME advisory services provided by specialized business support organizations;
➢ Training services to management teams of enterprises and local government officials and to target groups, such as unemployed persons, women and young people;
➢ Execution, administration and management of assistance programmes;
➢ Euro Advisory and Consulting services;
➢ Promotion of the regional and local economy.

Speakers from associated countries highlighted the crucial significance of regionally differentiated approaches and subsidiarity. Assistance funds are most efficiently and effectively employed, if channelled to regions, as regions differ in their resources and needs. Non-Governmental organizations, which have been working with local entrepreneurs for years, are best placed to know the needs of the region. In addition, weaker regions within countries require special support, as regional differences in SME development are present both in countries in transition and associated countries.

Employing a culturally sensitive public relations approach can play an important role in changing popular attitudes toward entrepreneurs, as was successfully demonstrated in Croatia. A good public-relations campaign can also be very effective in informing entrepreneurs about business support services available to them. Often managers of SMEs are unaware of what they need to improve their companies. The need for external consulting is not treated as a priority. In some countries or regions, these managers are not even aware that business advisory services exist for their companies.

Business services institutions in associated countries and countries in transition have integrated information technology into their services according to their capabilities. An encouraging example of the successful use of information technology in business advisory services has been the "web-site-shop," sponsored by the Moscow City Government, which uses a web site to provide information, online applications, and other advisory services to small businesses.

The area of standards, monitoring of quality and evaluation is largely underdeveloped in both associated countries and countries in transition, with some exceptions. In some countries, notably the Russian Federation and other countries in transition, although most of the existing business services institutions claim to be multifunctional, they employ no more than five or six people to provide a variety of services. Instead of occupying their own niche in the market, these entities are often in keen competition with each other and, as a result, contribute to an unfavourable business environment. Associated countries have adopted or are adopting EU quality standards, e.g. ISO 9000 and ISO 14000, but they require a reliable and transparent monitoring and evaluation system for business advisory, counselling and information services. In Poland, an important step has been taken in this direction by creating a comprehensive quality assurance system, including an elaboration of business consultancy ethics.

Speakers noted the need to provide a flexible range of services, adaptable to changing needs and a changing environment. Lack of access to external financing continues to be one of the most serious obstacles to SMEs in all countries despite the existence of financing institutions, which offer financing to SMEs. These are non-bank institutions, providing venture capital, loan funds and credit guarantee funds.

In all associated countries, services are offered by Euro Info Centres alongside those provided by other business services institutions. Although EICs occupy a niche in EU-related matters and contribute to SME internationalization, more coordination and synergy between various BSIs can preclude duplication of activities. In response to an inquiry about the possibility of setting up Euro Info Centres in non-associated countries in transition,

it became clear that the initiative for setting up a new Euro Info Centre needs reassurance from the Government. In terms of financing, a new EIC in countries in transition, one must examine the policy of the European Commission towards the respective country and opportunities within the TACIS Programme.

CHAPTER 8.
UNECE ROUND TABLE DISCUSSION ON THE SUSTAINABILITY OF BUSINESS SERVICES INSTITUTIONS

Mr Antal Szabo (UNECE) moderated the Round Table Discussion on Best Practice in Business Advisory, Counselling and Information Services. Discussion panellists were high-level policy makers (Ms Maja Tomani-Vidovi, State Secretary at the Ministry of Small Business and Tourism of Slovenia and Mr Anatoly Skorbezh, Minister for Entrepreneurship and Investments, Belarus); scientist (Mr Carlo Salvato, Professor at Cattaneo University, Castellanza, Italy); members of international organizations (Ms Lorraine Ruffing, UNCTAD and Ms Ewa Ruminska-Zimny, UNECE); representatives of NGOs (Ms Katarina Jagic, President of Small and Medium Entrepreneurs' Association of Croatia and Mr Alexandr Ioffe, President of the Russian Association for the Development of Small-sized Enterprises).

The following issues were discussed:

➤ Types of services to be provided and for which groups;
➤ First-stop-shop versus one-stop-shop services;
➤ Physical infrastructure versus virtual network;
➤ Financing of services:
  - to be subsidized or not?
  - who should pay (public/private) and at what rate?
➤ Quality standards:
  - which are the evaluation criteria?
  - how to evaluate the performance of BSIs?

- Competition amongst local BSIs and ways to overcome it;
- Ways to benefit from each other's experience and follow-up to this Meeting.

PART III
CURRENT SITUATION

CHAPTER 9.

CURRENT SITUATION IN UNECE MEMBER STATES

Azerbaijan

The development of small and medium-sized enterprises is one of the main priorities of the economic policy of the Government. The tool for the coordination of the structures supporting SME development and also for mobilizing resources to meet their needs are the governmental programmes for the development and support of SMEs. Today the discussions on the third SME development programme for the years 2001 – 2003 are being completed. The quantitative indicators prove that the SME sector is becoming one of the leading arenas where economic and social problems are being solved in the country.

However, current experience in Azerbaijan is rather related to revealing problem areas than to solving them effectively. This applies equally to the area of consulting services. Thus, the arrangements for a system of consulting enterprises have been reflected in all programmes. Obviously, all aspects of such infrastructure could not be addressed in a three-year period, which is the present programme cycle.

First, the problem of adequacy of consulting services in relation to the level of development and real needs of SMEs, as opposed to that in more advanced systems, is an issue that needs to be discussed within the context of transition. The transition process creates a whole new environment where consulting services need to be adapted to the needs of SMEs, and thus, the set-up of such services needs to be seen beyond national or local economies alone.

Secondly, as regards the transition economies, the development of a legal framework for SMEs goes much faster than development of an infrastructure such as consulting services for SMEs. Often, one can find serious discrepancies in the organization, functions and principles of such activities, even if they look similar on the surface. The problem of selecting the most effective infrastructure for consulting services has been the most difficult and disputed question in our discussions with our foreign partners as well as our domestic financial organizations.

Thirdly, the role of the Government in setting up an infrastructure for consulting services is principally different in advanced market economies and in countries with economies in transition. In addition, there is not even one variation for all transition economies either. For us, the most acceptable would be that the Government should mainly give direction and stimulate the process of creating an infrastructure for consulting services. However, it is understood that such an approach has some negative features, too. Particularly, the absence of generally available mechanisms (and specifically, the lack of human resources) can lead to man-made barriers blocking the development of a competitive business environment for consulting services.

In recent years, significant steps – both quantitative and structural – have been taken in the development of consulting services. As regards the structures, the process could be described as an expansion of the spectrum of specific legal services, financial credit consultation as well as in the area of production technologies.

Simultaneously, the process of specialization of the actual consulting structures takes place very slowly and there seems still to be a tendency to keep the old, rather undeveloped all-around services in the business going. In the end, this has a negative impact not only on the level of the effect of the services but also as regards the consolidation of such services. The public business organizations that have been created by the information, consulting and marketing companies do not seem to have an impact on the development of consulting services. The establishment of strong professional public associations seems to be awaited as a result of the Government's support activities, too.

During the past few years the number of SMEs that utilize the services of general and specialized consulting companies has grown significantly. Against this background, one has to take note of the following factors. First, in the number of services of consulting companies that are directly aimed at SMEs, the share of services rendered directly to enterprises is growing. Owing to some specific features in the country related to the prestige of consulting companies, the main sector has been left outside the focus of our SME development policy. At the same time, there are a growing number of companies that are already interesting for consulting companies. Although their number may be still somewhat limited, the variety of these companies is surprisingly wide. Together with other instruments, the Government's sectoral economic priorities as well as donor-funded foreign projects have a great stimulating role, despite the fact that the number of business people able to pay for consulting services is still a concern.

Thirdly, the SME sector – including a number of privatized enterprises – tends to feel that quality services in consulting are a factor that has a definite bearing on the competitiveness of a company.

Yet another problem is the regional disproportions as regards the development of an infrastructure for consulting services. In a situation where 75 % of SME activity is concentrated in the capital region, the economic and social aspects can be clearly seen. The authorities have in fact created over 40 regional enterprise development centres. These centres are independent legal entities that are hoped to be developed into general consulting services in the respective regions. Two issues of interest can be seen in this development. First, such centres can only be sustained if the initial inputs – both financial and intellectual – come from the outside. In the present set-up this is only feasible in cooperation with foreign partners. Secondly, the level of activity of the local and regional authorities is a success criterion, too. It has to be assumed that a tripartite arrangement at a regional level has to be formed with the participation of foreign partners, the Government and the local and regional authorities.

The problem of setting priorities for infrastructure development is critical not only at the level of political decision making but also at the level of concrete action. Currently, priorities may be different government offices implementing certain policies as opposed to those at the level of the Government's policy making.

In Azerbaijan, this issue is dealt with at an interministerial level and is part of the agenda of the interministerial coordination council on SMEs. However, it has not been possible even within such an interministerial structure to overcome the narrow approaches to solving these problems In practical terms, this means that neither the establishment of regional enterprise development centres nor the development of the necessary infrastructure for consulting services has become part of the priority areas where financial support to SMEs is allocated.

International, regional and foreign projects to support the development of consulting services have to support local efforts. Their resources should be used competitively and made available to the emerging consulting services. This is why an expansion of the group of users should be a condition sine qua non for any project and the coordination of project activities should take care not only of unnecessary duplication but also of the differentiation of potential local partners.

Partnerships between local consulting companies and transnationals are important both for strategic development and for the expansion of the markets. Although they may be completely different kinds of firm with very different goals, they may compete with each other in a certain market. Today, it is much more important for local consulting companies to develop cooperation and contacts with transnational companies at different levels.

Belarus

Today, private enterprises are one of the most dynamic sectors of the Belarusian economy. Non-government enterprises now account for 43% of the total industrial output. Small businesses, including sole traders, employ 446,000 people, which represent 9.5% of the work force. They produce 5% of the country's industrial output and account for over 30% of retail turnover.

Small businesses have always been the only growing sector of the economy. They have provided the highest rates of return on investment and have been an example of resource efficiency. Small businesses have absorbed a high proportion of the surplus work force from other sectors, thus alleviating numerous social problems

The available experience suggests that an effective State policy towards small business should be supported by a stable and comprehensive system of State support for private enterprise. The legislation that has been enacted to date has introduced the following basic components of such a system:

➤ Management and control (administered by the Ministry of Entrepreneurship and Investments);

➤ Financial support provided by the national and regional funds for financial support of entrepreneurs;

➤ Small business consulting and advice offered through a network of enterprise support centres, science parks and business incubators.

The Ministry of Entrepreneurship and Investments is the focal point for implementing the State policy on private enterprise and private sector investments. The Ministry is also responsible for measures to control monopolies, protect consumer rights and control advertising. In addition, it is in charge of all activities aimed at building a comprehensive small business support infrastructure and creating a conducive environment for small business development.

In its effort to implement State policy, the Ministry has drafted a number of laws and government decrees. For example, the law "On State Support for Small Business", adopted in October 1996, clarifies the main objectives of government support for private enterprise.

In line with the law, annual national and regional enterprise support programmes are adopted. The enterprise support infrastructure is instrumental in implementing these programmes as it serves as a channel for targeted financial support provided by the State to small business.

It is obvious that the work of enterprise support centres, business incubators and science parks is unique for every country. But the types of support provided to those institutions are quite similar, and include material, financial and institutional support, as well as information and advice. Nearly all of the services available at a business support institution are provided at a reduced cost to the client. Therefore, many components of such an infrastructure may experience serious difficulties, especially at the initial stages, as they often have to incur substantial costs that are too high for the institution to cover.

The case of the enterprise support centre "Belbusinesscentre" in Mozyr is a good example that illustrates this problem. The centre provides information, advice and consultancies to the local small business, thus contributing to the creation of a favourable environment for private enterprise in the community. The services provided by the centre include:

> Advice on starting up a business
> Access to market information from computer data bases
> Legal advice, help in drafting charter documents
> Advice on taxation, licensing and certification
> Education and professional training for small business owners, employees and sole traders
> Business planning.

The centre employs seven people. It is connected to the Internet, has access to e-mail and maintains a web page of its own. Although the centre's operational and staffing costs exceed its income, this difference is partly covered by public funds. The funding, provided by the State small business support programme, enables the centre to remain in operation and perform its functions.

In 1998, the joint programme of UNDP and the Government of Belarus aimed at creating a small business support and development infrastructure conducted a competition among small business incubator projects. The Mozyr enterprise support centre was one of the winners and received significant additional financial support, which enabled it to open a business incubator. Today, the incubator has seven tenants, operating in different lines of business, such as heating grid repair, wholesale trade, tourism, and even a driving school. In addition to premises, the incubator's tenants are provided with extensive information support and office equipment. They have also access to electronic databases on various aspects of commerce and law.

The centre also provides consulting services and advice on a case-by-case basis and tailored to the needs of the individual customer. It organizes short-term courses and seminars targeting audiences with different skills and ability levels and frequently also one-day seminars to address the most recent changes in commercial legislation.

The centre's services enable small businesses to avoid numerous obstacles and errors at the growth stage and make them more likely to achieve success in the future. A customer's first visit to the centre's consultant is free of charge. During this first visit, a consultant makes an assessment of the customer's problems and needs, and drafts a service contract.

In addition to its direct function – helping business start-ups – the services for emerging small businesses also contribute to job creation and local economic development. The joint UNDP and Government of Belarus programme on creating a small business support and development infrastructure has also launched business incubation activities. The programme's consultants have researched and analysed the international experience in business incubation and drafted recommendations on how to establish and manage business incubators and provided technical assistance.

A legal entity that has acquired the status of an enterprise support centre is eligible for:

> funding under specific State programmes
> low-interest loans from enterprise support funds
> premises and office equipment for locating the centre; reductions or exemptions from rent and public utilities payments
> other funding and support in accordance with the existing legislation.

The power to provide an entity with the business incubator status or to deprive it of such a status rests with the Ministry of Entrepreneurship and Investments, which bases its decisions on applicable procedures and issues the required certificates.

Work is almost complete on establishing a national enterprise promotion agency. The concept, work methods, goals, objectives and structure of the new agency have been discussed with all interested parties and organizations. The agency's primary objective will be to help implement State policy on small and medium-sized enterprises and to coordinate the efforts of small business support institutions. The agency also serves as a centre for the research and analysis of issues related to small business development in Belarus.

Information services are an important component of enterprise support in Belarus. Information and marketing systems, along with trained personnel, are important prerequisites of the sustainable development of SMEs. Economic reforms and foreign investment are impossible without access to reliable and up-to-date information.

The global market information network, based at the Ministry of Entrepreneurship and Investments, has been the first real step in this direction. The market information network receives data from 48 market information centres in Belarus and more than 450 similar centres in the CIS. This system, called Teleinternet, operates as a global network of Intranet web-servers, which receive information through television channels. It is integrated into the Internet and other marketing information networks.

Teleinternet has the lowest cost of data transfer of all communication channels available in Belarus. Data is transferred to users through a system of personalised television modems. The regional network of web servers is also accessible through the Internet. Teleinternet carries several databases on the supply and demand for goods and services within the CIS, projects, partnership opportunities, technologies and innovation projects. Commercial proposals and information requests are transferred to all servers within the network within 24 hours. It is also relayed to other marketing information networks in the CIS and global Internet servers.

The Centre for Science and Innovation is the focal point for information exchange within the Teleinternet system. It provides connections to Belarusian companies and organizations wishing to access market information networks within the CIS. Through Teleinternet users can have the following information:

➢ Commercial proposals, requests for goods and services
➢ Announcements and results of tenders and auction sales
➢ Export/import opportunities
➢ New technologies and investment projects
➢ Directory of manufacturers and economic entities in Belarus.

Companies can place their commercial proposals on the net. This information is relayed to the 145 market information centres of the X-MIR network, 128 centres within the Relcom system, 21 centres in the IC-TPC network, 45 centres in the Interregional Network of Market Centres, 56 centres in the market information network of the Russian enterprise support agency, 48 centres in the marketing information network in Belarus, as well as the open-access Internet and Teleinternet servers. The eighth session of the CIS Advisory Council for Enterprise Support in Kiev in October 1999 adopted a programme to establish an intra-CIS system of information and advisory support for small business. This system should expand the access of small business throughout the CIS to global information resources and strengthen their position in local and CIS markets. The work of this system is based on the mutual exchange of data and data banks on various aspects of enterprise support.

The benefits of this new intra-CIS system are as follows:
➢ Participating States will be able to consolidate the resources and efforts of small business. They also benefit from the improved conditions for intra-CIS trade and greater opportunities for partnership between various enterprises within and outside their countries
➢ Business people will have less difficulty finding new partners and testing their trustworthiness. They will also gain access to professional advice and credit opportunities within the CIS and new markets. SMEs get real opportunities to

establish joint ventures, expand production and introduce advanced technologies.

Work on this system has been included in the national enterprise support programmes and is being regarded as a step towards intra-CIS integration. In some participating States, this system is being implemented as a part of their State or government programmes. Further development of TELEINTERNET will result in the emergence of an e-trade system, a distance-learning network for small businessmen and deeper integration into other information systems within the CIS.

Croatia

The Croatian Small and Medium-Sized Entrepreneurs' Association (SMEA) is an independent, non-profit, non-Governmental organization created in 1998 to promote small to medium-sized business enterprises throughout Croatia. SMEA is an organization created by entrepreneurs for entrepreneurs, its membership represents entrepreneurs and owners of small and medium-sized companies that have 1 – 250 employees.

The mission of SMEA is to link Croatian entrepreneurs to a domestic and international business network and to provide technical and legal assistance to entrepreneurs. SMEA lobbies the Government for a better economic environment for small and medium-sized enterprises.

SMEA has also created partnerships with a number of local, regional and national institutions and authorities, such as the Ministry for Crafts, Small and Medium Entrepreneurship, the Croatian Employment Office, the town and county of Rijeka and the county of Primorsko-Goranska as well as the Porin business centre in Rijeka.

Its international partners include the National Agency for Small and Medium-Sized Entrepreneurship Development, as well as the Slovak and Albanian Euro Info Centres.

The information services of SMEA include:
➢ access to sources of information on EU matters and EU programmes
➢ access to information on commercial, technological, production and financial cooperation with companies in the European Union
➢ Information for SMEs about supporting events
➢ information about Croatian SMEs

The SMEA counselling and advisory services include:
➢ assistance in international negotiations
➢ translation
➢ informatization by including information about SMEs' on web site and providing free of charge e-mail addresses
➢ matchmaking SMEs in Croatia
➢ promotion of health and safety in the workplace
➢ helping SMEs to resolve infrastructure problems
➢ promotion of SME members

SMEA has also produced a new customized tool, a software kit for SMEs with three modules for everyday operationalization of SMEs' business based on networking and modern computer technologies. It can be downloaded free of charge from the SMEA website (Croatian pages) www.odisej.hr/umis

SMEA is a member of the "Bureau de Rapprochement des Entreprises" network, which is an initiative of the European Commission with a central database of SMEs designed for partner search with 500 members in 74 countries. 223 Croatian SME company profiles are included.

A current pilot project of SMEA will produce a CD-ROM based on Dr. Milan Juranovic's patented methodology for a game on enterprise economics. It contains three disciplines: economics, management and accounting. The game is based on a simulation of business transactions.

Czech Republic

In the non-primary sector in the Czech Republic, i.e. all private enterprises except those in agriculture, forestry and fishing, SMEs cover enterprises employing less than 250 employees. Non-primary sector private companies employing 250 or more employees are regarded as large-scale enterprises.

Statistical indicators document well the significance of SMEs for the economy of the Czech Republic. In 1999 SMEs in industry, building, trade, service business, and other branches employed 59.1% of the total number of employees. Their share of the output of the above branches was 53.5 and in value added 53%. The share of SMEs in the exports out of the GDP was 38.9% of the total output of the Czech Republic.

The present SME policy was defined in the "SME support policy in 1999-2000" and acknowledged by the Government in their Act No. 562 from 9th June 1999. The policy draws on the conclusions of the 2nd National Conference of SMEs in Prague in April 2000 as well as on the recommendations of the National Discussion Group, a consultative body of the Ministry of Industry and Trade. The SME policy defines the role of the Government as regards work related to:
- EU accession
- the economic role of SMEs
- the extent and form of regulation and state intervention to enforce national policy goals, including institutional set-up and financing.

In the long term the SME policy should contribute to a better performance of the national economy and an increase in competitive advantage, e.g. through reduced employment.

In the medium term the policy goals are to:
- stimulate growth of the economy, including exports and, particularly, in structurally handicapped and economically weak regions

- increase the competitive advantage of SMEs, also with a view to their successful integration into EU markets
- facilitate people's access to entrepreneurship
- harmonize the tools and mechanisms for SME promotion in line with EU rules and to rationalize the mechanisms for their administration
- update and monitor implementation of the SME policy
- differentiate the support tools and their use in accordance with the different goals in different regions and branches:
  1. start-up entrepreneurs entering the business scene for the first time
  2. newly created enterprises (up to 2 years) without any previous business activity
  3. existing SMEs which are capable of applying for commercial financing resources
- differentiate projects
  o with lower level of innovation
  o with high level of innovation, high return potential and enhanced risk.

The current regulatory framework for SME support financed with budget funds is set in the Act No. 299/1992 "About the support to SMEs" and in the Act No 218/2000 "About budgetary rules" and Act No 59/2000 "About public support". A Novella of the Act No 299/1992 is being prepared and will be harmonised in accordance with EU legislation.

Business Service Institutions

SME affairs belong under the competence of the Ministry of Industry and Trade. In addition, however, two other ministries have particular interest in SME development, viz. the Ministry of Regional Affairs, which is responsible for regional support and development strategies and the Ministry of Labour and Social Affairs primarily concerned with unemployment. In addition, support tools related to access to capital are supplied through the Bohemian and Moravian Guarantee and Development Bank (BMGDB).

The Business Development Agency (BDA) was established as a Government body to implement the PHARE SME programme in the country. In 1995 it was transformed into a non-profit organization set up in accordance with the Act No. 229/1992 about the support of SME. As a semi-Governmental body, it is partially financed by the Ministry of Industry and Trade from the State budget.

During the last eight years BDA has become a specific institution covering several activities. Its principal activities are:

➤ Advisory and information services and innovation promotion. BDA initiated the establishment of the national network of Regional Advisory and Information Centres (RAIC) and Business Innovation Centres (BIC)

➤ Financial schemes - non-banking programme

In the Government's development plans for the future, the BDA is also envisaged to carry out a number of activities, such as:

➤ monitoring the business environment

➤ evaluating the effect of the SME support systems

➤ coordinating activities and financing the network of RAICs and BICs

➤ providing advantageously priced technical assistance services including counselling, information and education services for SMEs.

Furthermore, cooperation with chambers of commerce and business associations will be developed and a national discuss Group (NDG) will be set up as an advisory body to the Ministry of Industry and Trade. It will be composed of representatives of the Economic chamber, business and entrepreneurs' associations, representatives of industrialists and the State administration, with the BDA as the secretariat.

Euro Info Centres are well in place and provide a range of services, notably, information and consultation supporting the development of cooperation of SMEs with other European Union member countries.

Czech Trade is gradually widening its network of information centres within the country abroad. The objective is to achieve a level comparable with more advanced European countries and to contribute to the increase in the exports of high-value-added goods and services produced in the country.

The Czech agency for foreign investment, CZECHINVEST, is a national development agency whose task is to promote the country as an advantageous location in Europe for direct foreign investment in production and strategic services. It has a network of 14 regional agents in the country and 5 foreign representatives in three European countries, the United States and Japan.

Czech national network of RAICs and BICs a network of advisory centres for SMEs has been in operation since 1992. This network consists of:

➤ RAICs that form the National Business Development Association (NBDA)

➤ Business and Innovation Centres (BICs) that cooperate in the framework of the Czech National Committee of EBN.

The RAICs cover practically the entire country. In June 2000 the number of RAICs increased to 30. The first Czech BICs were established in 1991. They are private firms as well, except the BIC of the Czech Technical University in Prague. Since 1992, five Business and Innovation Centres have been opened in big cities. In addition to consultancy services, BICs provide space for innovative business incubators.

From the very beginning RAICs and BICs offered more affordable prices to their clients for counselling services, thanks to the financial subsidies received from the Czech Government and the PHARE programme.

Table 1: Selection Criteria

Critera:	Specifications:
1. Legal Form	Legal person in accordance with the Commercial Code
2. Main Activities Registered in the Commercial Register	Economic activities and organizational counsellors
3. Spheres of consulting activities	Economic consultancy (obligatory) A minimum of two of the following: - accounting - taxes - commercial law - marketing - management - quality - other business consultancies
4. Experience in business consulting	Minimum of 2 years
5. Minimum number of employees	3 professional advisors (full time or associates)
6. External cooperation	Cooperation with external advisors and capability to secure advisory services in further spheres
7. Spheres of activity	Primarily small and medium-sized enterprises and individuals
8. Current cooperation or readiness for cooperation with regional authorities	District Office, Municipal and Local Offices, Trade Office, Labour Office, Chambers of Economy, other business organizations
9. References	At least from 5 customers or business projects, applications for credit etc prepared and implemented
10. Technical equipment	PCs, SW: Windows 95/NT, MS Office Professional, access to Internet, e-mail, homepage, printer, copier, fax, telephone.

Table 2 Growth of the National networks of RAICs and BICs

YEAR	NETWORK					Total RAIC/BIC
	RAIC		BIC			
	Change in number	Total	Change in number	Total		
1992	5	5	3	3		8
1993	14	19		3		22
1994	-1	18		3		21
1995	-1	17		3		20
1996	-1	16	2	5		21
1997	7	23		5		28
1998	-1	22		5		27
1999	-1	21		5		26
2000	9	30		5		35

Table 3:   Summary of services provided by RAICs and BICs (1997-1999)

COP 97 Service	1997		1998		1999		Subtotal		Total RAIC/BIC
	RAIC	BIC	RAIC	BIC	RAIC	BIC	RAIC	BIC	
Introductory consultations	6062	827	340	59	840	200	7242	1086	8328
Specialist advisory services	2568	424	180	15	341	21	3089	460	3549
Support of innovative firms in incubator	0	108	0	23	0	32	0	163	163
Number of training courses	223	75	11	0	29	1	263	76	339
Number of participants in the training	5123	718	300	0	725	15	6148	733	6881
Advisory services for regional authorities for SME development	90	10	6	0	12	1	108	11	119

Originally, RAICs were founded based on the Government decision No.9/1992 that requires the agreement of district councils. However, the RAICs and BICs can provide services for clients outside their respective territories, too.

RAICs are private firms established according to the Commercial Code. BICs are private firms as well, except the BIC at the Technical University of Prague. The European Business and Innovation Centre Network prepared the standard approach (Vade Mecum etc.), used by the Czech BICs. The BDA in cooperation with NBDA will prepare a manual on the management of subsidized advisory services for SMEs in cooperation with NBDA and CNC EBN.

Criteria for the establishment of business advisory, counselling and information services

Selective conditions for the expansion of the RAIC network RAIC.

The RAIC and BIC consultants have been professionally trained. Between 1992 and 1994, 18 consultants and managers of RAICs and BICs were trained at the Durham University Business School and after that a number of courses in advisory procedures, crisis management,

marketing and international business were provided. Some employees of the advisory centres have also passed the exams for accounting auditors and tax advisors.

Experts of the European Business and Innovation Network have trained directors and staff of BICs in specific services, provided by BICs.

The creation of first RAICs and BICs was supported by the PHARE programme with a total of 20 million Euros. Additional financial resources were allocated to the existing RAICs and BICs and for the extension of the network. In 1998, the PHARE Cross-Border Cooperation programme with Germany included a component related to advisory services to Czech SMEs and has involved 5 RAICs and 1 BIC, and the project is also linked to the Programme of Support for Consultancy services for SMEs, which was cofinanced from the Czech State budget. German bilateral cooperation has also contributed to the financing of RAICs.

Segmentation of contributions and their content:
  ➢ Contribution towards favourable prices of services for entrepreneurs
  ➢ Counselling and consulting activities.
    This type of service includes:
  ➢ introductory consultations to provide basic information to entrepreneurs, to be provided by a RAIC or a BIC
  ➢ specialist advisory services including the preparation of business plans and implementation projects, to be provided by a RAIC or a BIC.

The purpose of the introductory consultation is to analyse the problem of the entrepreneur and to provide basic information. The introductory consultation has to be clear, brief and prepared in a standard manner.

The specialist counselling services include advice in the areas of:
  ➢ general management (corporate strategy, management structure and systems, corporate culture and management style, innovation and business activities)
  ➢ management (company assessment, control, investment analysis, financial analysis, preparation of business plans, financial management, accounting systems, use of management systems, etc.)
  ➢ marketing and sales management (marketing strategy, operations, international marketing, etc.)
  ➢ production management (production methods and organization, management production computerised tools, etc.)
  ➢ human resource management (planning of human resources, motivation and remuneration systems, etc.).

The services are based on a standard set of:

➢ basic information on business
➢ information on SME support
➢ counselling on how to establish a company
➢ counselling on the development of a business plan
➢ counselling on the financing of business
➢ marketing counselling
➢ management counselling
➢ requalification course "Business base/ business minimum".

Mutual products also include:

➢ crisis management
➢ cost management
➢ mediation of cooperation
➢ financial schemes for SMEs.

The support of innovative firms through BIC Incubators covers rent, operating expenses (electricity, water, etc.) and other necessary rent-related services, which are specified exactly in the agreement between BIC and the beneficiary company, which is subsidized by the project.

Table 4: Contribution towards the services for SMEs in 1999, through RAICs and BICs

		Maximum rate	*Contribution (Excluding VAT)*
A	Contribution towards favourable prices of services for entrepreneurs		
A 1	Counselling and consultation activities	CZK 40.000/1 SME	
A 1.1	Introductory consultation (max. 3 hours)	CZK 400/hour	100%
A 1.2	Specialist advisory services		
A 1.2.1	Start-up micro firms (less than 10 employees)	CZK 500/hour	60%
A 1.2.2	Other SMEs (less than 250 employees)	CZK 500/hour	40%
A 2	Support of innovative production firms in BIC Incubators	CZK 2.400/1 m2	as per price shown
		1. year	50%
		2. year	40%
		3. year	30%
A 3	Training of entrepreneurs	as per price shown	60%
A 4	Crisis management		
A 4.1	BDA products (Small Loan, Obnova projects, Technos, etc.)	max. CZK 500/hour, CZK 18.000/1 SME	100%
B	Specialist advisory services for State institutions and regional authorities aimed at the development of SME sector		
B 1	Analysis, strategies, development projects etc.	max. CZK 500/hour, CZK 80.000/1 organization	45%
C	Contribution towards the improvement of RAIC/BIC services		
C 1	Membership fees to international organizations, chamber of commerce etc.	as per price shown	100%
C 2	Seminars, training actions, exhibitions, promotion RAIC/BIC	as per price shown	40%
C 3	Participation to specialized events	as per price shown	100%
C 4	Internet access fees	as per price shown, CZK 30.000/1 year	100%
C 5	Purchase of software and professional literature	as per price shown	40%
C 6	Audit of documents for PHARE contribution	as per price shown, CZK 25.000	100%
C 7	Costs of implementation and certification of ISO 9000		
C 7.1	Level of contribution for current RAIC/BIC certified by 31.3.2001 and for new RAIC/BIC certified in 1 year	max. 50.000 CZK / RAIC or BIC	40%

			Maximum rate	Contribution (Excluding VAT)
C 7.2	Level of contribution for current RAIC/BIC certified by 30.9.2001 and for new RAIC/BIC certified in 1.5 year (if next contract possible)		max. 30.000 CZK / RAIC or BIC	20%
C 8	Contribution to costs of contact places		max CZK 100.000	50%
D	Support of RAIC and BIC networks (Experiment financed from BDA budget)			
D 1	Costs of software, informatics and communication			100%
D 2	Presentation and didactic equipment for temporary lending for use by all members of the networks			100%
	Share of each section	A		50%
	(enlargement of a share is possible only for the benefit of section A)	B		20%
		C		30%
		D		
		Total		100%

The training of entrepreneurs includes basic as well as specialist training for SME management, start-up business, re-qualification, organized by the RAICs and BICs.

The crisis management services include preventive expertise focused on the identification of problems, where an analysis of the present situation is made and a feasible curative process identified.

Special advisory services related to SME development are rendered to State institutions and regional authorities (including legal associations of municipalities representing a Czech region, towns and villages, local authorities and regional development agencies). They include designing and implementing regional development programmes for small and medium entrepreneurs.

As part of improving their service base, the operational costs of producing certain services are reimbursed to the RAICs and BICs, and particularly:

 ➤ membership fees to international organizations and chambers of commerce and other entrepreneurial associations, upon prior approval by BDA

 ➤ training courses for the permanent staff of RAICs and BICs, including language training
 ➤ participation of RAICs and BICs in specialized exhibitions and fairs
 ➤ participation of RAICs and BICs in specialized events organized by BDA and, as appropriate, the Government or European Commission bodies
 ➤ promotion of RAICs and BICs
 ➤ fees related to the implementation of ISO 9000 at RAICs and BICs
 ➤ accreditation and certification by BDA
 ➤ Internet access fees
 ➤ "contact place" operations for RAICs and BICs (rent, wages)
 ➤ translation and interpreting services
 ➤ purchase of software and professional literature.

The Science and Technology Parks Association of the Czech Republic (STPA)

This association was established on July 27, 1990. It is a union of private persons, technology centres, business and innovation centres, and science and technology parks.

The principal aims of the STPA include:
 ➤ more flexible transfer of scientific and research results into industry,

- achievement of better competitiveness in both domestic and foreign markets,
- strengthening of promising, technically progressive production programmes to replace outdated and inefficient processes, gradually leading to structural changes in the economy, especially in problematic regions,
- revitalization of the economy in certain regions by creating employment opportunities,
- establishment and creation of small and medium-sized innovation companies,
- domestic and international cooperation.

Association of Innovative Entrepreneurship of the Czech Republic (AIE CR)

Since 1993, the Association of Innovative Entrepreneurship of the Czech Republic is a non-government organization in the field of innovative entrepreneurship. It is a union of natural persons nominated by the Science and Technology Parks Association, Society for Technology Transfer Support, Czech Society for New Materials and Technologies or by other domestic or foreign subjects that take part in development of the innovative entrepreneurship in the Czech Republic.

The objectives of the AIE CR are to create prerequisites for the development of innovative entrepreneurship, i.e. research and development, technology transfer, new materials and technologies, building of science and technology parks (science parks and centres, business and innovation centres), and support the activities of innovative firms. The main aim is to create an innovative infrastructure, an innovative market and functional technology exchange.

Standardization and certification of business support institutions

The preparation and implementation of ISO 9000 including the quality of a standard set of advisory services was based on a network that will be organized by the BDA and BDNA/EBN.

Professional firms will manage quality training and the related costs will be subsidized for up to 20 – 40% of the actual costs (up to a maximum of 30,000 – 50,000 CZK) for each RAIC or BIC if the RAIC or BIC in question is certified by 31 March 2001 or 31 September 2001 respectively. If additional funds can be allocated, the activity will be continued beyond September 2001.

The training in quality management systems will enable RAICS to participate in the implementation of the "national quality" policy in the regions.

The Role of Information Technology in Entrepreneurship Development: experience with One-stop shops

The objective of Czech policy is to guarantee the availability of the necessary information for the establishment of a business and the operating and controlling activities of enterprises.

For this, Euro Info Centres as a part of the European network will be established and will undertake support activities to integrate SME into e-markets.

Finland

The aim of SME policy is to promote small and medium-sized businesses and entrepreneurship development, and thus improve employment as well as competitiveness and economic growth in society. The main responsibility for SME policy lies with the Ministry of Trade and Industry (MTI), which implements policy in cooperation with other relevant ministries and organizations. In Finland the general objectives can be divided into the following categories (MTI 1996, KTM 1999):
- Improving the operating environment for SMEs
- Improving the working conditions of SMEs
- Improving the growth and competitiveness of SMEs.

The first objective includes areas such as the simplification of licensing procedures and the evaluation of the effects of regulations and laws on SMEs. Finnish SME policy has focused on the improvement of the operating environment in recent years. In this work, efforts to reduce the administrative burden have been the central issue.

The second objective is connected with the activities of the Economic and Development Centres (under the MTI), as well as the Ministry of Education. In 1997 the regional offices of three ministries – Ministry of Trade and Industry, Ministry of Labour and Ministry of Agriculture – were merged. These 15 Employment and Economic Development Centres (EEDC) operate as one-stop-shops in the regions to improve employment and to homogenize regional decision-making in the fields of labour and enterprise policy.

The Government has a specific programme for SME and entrepreneurship development, aiming at strengthening entrepreneurship and the growth of SMEs as well as competitiveness and creating new jobs.

Some of the goals of the programme include removing barriers to business operations and encouraging all administrative branches to promote the establishment of new companies. The programme has also set the prerequisites for the fair treatment of companies in different fields regarding taxation and payments as well as company subsidies, including the possibility for small companies to collect tax at source and make social security contributions in one payment and to promote change-of-generation in family firms

The administrative burden of SMEs can be alleviated by improving the opportunities for small enterprises to do their business using electronic data transfer and combining the collection of data required by various authorities.

Special public funding will be made more effective by filling those gaps in the market, and financial services that will promote and develop the internationalization of small and medium-sized enterprises. Export companies will be guaranteed internationally competitive financial services.

The Government's support for companies aims at improving their ability to operate, taking into account the demands for balanced regional development. The Government is developing its subsidy system by improving the follow-up and monitoring of support programmes. For instance, evaluation of the effectiveness of financial support will be enhanced.

In the years 1998 – 2000, the Ministry of Trade and Industry made four surveys regarding the views of entrepreneurs on the organizations promoting entrepreneurship. The study is based on the subjective view of the entrepreneurs of how these organizations succeed in promoting entrepreneurship. The last of these studies was made in the spring of 2000 with 4,000 small and medium-sized entrepreneurs taking part.

In the survey, the entrepreneurs' familiarity with the different organizations and the use of these organizations during the previous year was examined. In the results, it appears, understandably, that the familiarity with and the use of services correlates strongly but not fully. There are remarkable differences as to how many times certain services have been used. For instance, services focusing on a special restricted aspect of entrepreneurship or on a very small range of entrepreneurs were less used.

The entrepreneurs' familiarity with any particular organization or how often the organization's services were used, does not seem to depend on whether it is publicly financed or a private organization, but both kinds can be found amongst the best known and well-used organizations as well as in the less known and less utilized organizations. What seems to be essential is that the functions be focused on enterprises and not on some aspects of entrepreneurship only. The same conclusions have been arrived at in some earlier studies conducted by the Ministry, and the views seem to be rather stable with small variations.

In the study, the entrepreneurs also evaluated the success of the different organizations as promoters of an enabling environment for SMEs. Supposedly, the organizations whose services were often used would receive a better evaluation. The results confirm the pattern, although some relatively significant changes in the individual evaluations of certain organizations can be found. Clearly, the best assessments were given to public educational services and to organizations representing entrepreneurs. Public – municipal and regional – services and centres promoting entrepreneurship, received poorer grades.

Even if the results reflect the subjective view of the entrepreneurs, the results of the earlier studies were very similar to those of the 2000 study. Thus, the view of the entrepreneurs seems to be rather stable. How well the different organizations have been able to influence the development of entrepreneurship is very difficult to measure. If the stable view of the entrepreneurs of the importance of the different organizations is real, the answers are very interesting. The best yield for promoting entrepreneurship according to this, would come from the voluntary industrial organizations and from publicly financed educational services established for entrepreneurial purposes, whereas the publicly financed consultative organizations seem relatively inefficient. As a matter of fact, public investments in this domain have been directed towards education and the financing of special advisory and entrepreneurship promoting organizations. Consequently, the practical support seems to correspond with the subjective views presented by the entrepreneurs in the study.

Business Service Institutions

Institutions promoting entrepreneurship can be defined as organizations expressly founded with public funds to promote entrepreneurship. More widely, organizations important to entrepreneurship also include private institutions promoting entrepreneurship and educational systems promoting entrepreneurship. In the following, organizations promoting entrepreneurship are defined according to this wider concept.

Federation of Finnish Enterprises (FFE)

The Federation of Finnish Enterprises covers small and medium-sized enterprises. Its main goals include the reduction of administrative bureaucracy and the easing of taxation. The Federation also concerns itself with labour legislation and local labour agreements. Particular areas of activity also relate to the position of the sole entrepreneur and social security of entrepreneurs and their families. FFE offers advisory services to its members on issues such as corporate taxation, corporate law, labour legislation, business financing, contract law, patents, internationalization, and the social security of entrepreneurs.

The Central Chamber of Commerce

The Central Chamber of Commerce in Finland, together with 21 chambers of commerce, make up the Finnish organization that looks after the general interests of business and industry, as well as promoting the basic operating conditions of companies regionally, nationally and within the European Union, particularly relating to matters of taxation, legislation, economic policy, SME policy, regional and structural policy, trade policy and EU policy. The chambers of commerce have over 14,700 company and organization members.

The Confederation of Finnish Industry and Employers and the Employers' Confederation of Service Industries in Finland

The Confederation of Finnish Industry and Employers (TT) with a membership of some 5,600 enterprises employing 470,000 people safeguards the interests of companies in manufacturing, construction, transport and other services related to industry. The Confederation represents its members in business and industrial, economic, trade and social policy.

The Employers' Confederation in the Service Industries of Finland (PT) is the central employer organization of private service industries and the guardian of the interests of its member enterprises in all labour-related matters, trade and community policy-making.

In the autumn of 1999 the membership of the Confederation numbered approximately 8,200 enterprises, employing about 330,000 persons.

Finnvera

Finnvera is a specialized financing company with a twofold task. On the one hand, it promotes exports by offering export credit guarantees and on the other, it supports domestic small and medium-sized companies by offering risk financing and guarantees. Owned entirely by the Government, Finnvera was formed in 1999 by merging the activities of two former State financing bodies, the Kera Corporation and the Finnish Guarantee Board (FGB). Finnvera has a national network with 15 regional offices.

Tekes – the National Technology Agency

The primary objective of the National Technology Agency is to promote the competitiveness of Finnish industries and the service sector through technological innovation. Its activities aim at diversifying production structures, increasing productivity and potential for exports, as well as generating employment and social well being.

The core functions are:
➢ preparation of the national technology policy
➢ preparation, financing and coordination of national technology programmes
➢ financing applied technical research and risk-intensive industrial R&D projects
➢ financing and coordination of international technological cooperation

➢ providing SME advisory services in technology transfer and exploitation

Finpro

Finpro (formerly the Finnish Foreign Trade Association) is a service organization helping entrepreneurs and enterprises in their international operations, particularly in the process of internationalization with a particular view to minimizing the risks involved. Finpro is a joint private - public sector organization, partly financed from public funds. It works in cooperation with other Finnish service organizations working towards the same goals. It offers services to companies at all stages of their internationalization.

Venture Capital Companies

There are about 40 venture capital companies in Finland. In 1999 they made 325 investments totalling Euro 300 million. The share of public venture capital amounted to 18%, arranged by publicly owned investors.

Euro Info Centres

Finland has 14 Euro Info Centres. They provide information and advice and encourage companies to participate in the different programmes of the European Commission. They also train and advise in all EU related matters that SMEs may encounter.

Municipal and Regional Services

Municipal and regional services are provided in many different ways. In many cases, they are provided by companies owned by municipalities themselves. In some cases the municipality in question has these activities in its own organization. The main tasks of these services, no matter how organized, include
➢ advice for start-ups
➢ advice to existing enterprises
➢ networking and project development

- ➢ support with premises for industry and new (hi-tech) enterprises
- ➢ risk-financing

Employment and Economic Development Centres

EEDCs provide services to businesses, farmers and individuals in 15 regions in Finland. They promote employment and entrepreneurship development through increased competitiveness and growth of companies as part of the current regional policy in the country. They advise and support SMEs during all phases of their development.

Polytechnics

There are 29 polytechnics in Finland, most of them are multidisciplinary, regional institutes, which give particular weight to contacts with business and industry. Polytechnics are developed as part of the national and international higher education system, with special emphasis on their expertise in technical skills required in working life. The polytechnics also carry out research and development projects relevant to their teaching.

The polytechnics award professionally oriented higher education degrees, which take three to four years to accomplish. The entry requirements are either an upper secondary school certificate or a vocational diploma. At present, about 70% of all entrants are upper secondary school graduates and 30% vocational graduates.

Polytechnic education is provided in the following fields:
- ➢ Natural resources
- ➢ Technology and transport
- ➢ Administration and business
- ➢ Hotel, catering and home economics
- ➢ Health and social services
- ➢ Culture
- ➢ Humanities and education

University education

Finland has 20 universities: ten multi-faculty ones, three universities of technology, three schools of economics and business administration and four art academies. Geographically, the network covers the whole country. All universities are State-run, with the Government providing some 70% of their funding. Universities select their own students and the competition for openings is stiff.

Adult Education Centres

Adult education and training is available in over 1,000 institutions. Some of these provide education and training only for adults, but the majority cater for both young people and adults. Adult education is arranged by universities and polytechnics, public and private vocational institutions, adult education centres and summer universities, upper secondary schools with adult sections, study centres, sports institutes and music institutes. These establishments provide adult education and training to about one million students each year, amounting to some 10 million classroom hours. In all publicly funded institutions, tuition is free for the students. For other institutions, students pay either a subsidized fee or the market price.

Networking among Business Service Institutions

Cooperation between the publicly financed entrepreneurship promoting organizations, such as EEDCs, Finnvera, Tekes, Finpro and the Euro Info Centres is based on different mutual agreements leading to a more efficient use of resources. A whole new possibility that is opening up for such cooperation is the Internet, directed to the promotion of entrepreneurship. With the help of the Internet, enterprises can be in contact with a group of different entrepreneurship-promoting organization

Germany

Businesses in Germany have a tightly woven network of information, consulting and support resources at their disposal: chambers of industry and commerce, chambers of handicrafts, State-backed institutions, and regional, district and municipal economic development departments. Each of these organizations provides unique services and fulfils a clearly defined function within the overall network of economic development, business information and business consulting services.

The German chambers of industry and commerce operate on behalf of the more than three million companies which they represent, and they are thus the country's biggest and most potent force for business advisory, counselling and information services.

Germany itself has 82 chambers of industry and commerce, and there are 49 chambers abroad and 20 further representative and proxy offices. The chambers employ a total of 6,600 specialists in fields such as company and tax law, environment, trade and industry, vocational education, and arbitrators for the settlement of disputes. Some 250,000 staff from member companies also work for the chamber organization in an honorary capacity and serve on chamber committees.

Chambers of industry and commerce

Today, successful businesspeople have to be more abreast of developments than ever before. The Government creates a complex regulatory framework for entrepreneurial activity; and things can change very quickly. But the Government does more than just fix the ground rules: it also helps itself to a sizable portion of private and corporate income to cover its own expenditures. In order to keep the State's regulatory powers and tax demands in check and constantly be informed of developments, the business community needs strong representative bodies. These are the chambers of industry and commerce.

Structure

All commercial companies are required by law to be members of the chamber of industry and commerce in their region. Mandatory membership has many advantages. The chambers represent all industries and all companies of whatever size, from the "mom-and-pop" store to the large multinational. Every member has one vote, and all have the same rights. This makes the chambers both independent and neutral, since they are compelled to maintain a balance of interests between companies and between different branches of industry. All companies pay a compulsory subscription fee in line with their economic capabilities. The chambers therefore require no public funding and are independent of government influence. This leaves them free to vigorously represent the interests of their members.

The chambers have a democratic structure. The members elect their representatives to the General Assembly, which in turn elects the president, the vice-president and the chief executive officer. Each company has one vote. The president of a chamber must always be a businessperson.

Functions

The chambers of industry and commerce have three functions: they discharge public duties imposed on them by their statutory mandate and administered autonomously by the chambers on behalf of industries; they represent interest groups and provide policy advice at federal, State and local (municipal) levels; and they provide an extensive range of advisory and other services.

Administrative tasks

The chambers are public bodies with a status accorded by the Government because they perform public functions more cheaply and effectively than the Government itself would be able to do.

The public duties assumed by the chambers (and on which they also provide detailed information and advice to businesses) are varied. For example, 7,000 sworn experts appointed by the chambers prepare reports and advisory opinions in about 200 different fields for the courts, public authorities and private clients. Licences for more than 100 trades and professions are subject to chamber reports. For instance, the chamber must assess a person's character and, in some cases, their professional knowledge and ability before the person is allowed to start up a business. In exceptional cases, e.g. during trade shows and exhibitions, when restrictions on shop opening and closing times can be changed, consultation with the local chamber is mandatory. The chambers also help the local courts maintain a commercial register. They make sure that new entries do not create confusion with existing ones, or that a firm's name does not give a false impression of its business activities. They oversee clearance and closing-down sales to make sure these do not infringe on competition regulations. The chambers in Germany also register companies for the European Environmental Management and Audit Scheme.

Another task is to train skilled workers and specialists. The chambers help with training and, at the same time, inform young people about professional opportunities and promote recruitment. Germany has a dual system of vocational training, i.e. a combination of learning-on-the-job and attending part-time vocational school. It ensures high standards and thus helps maintain the quality of products.

The chambers play an important part in the dual training system. They advise firms on training courses, provide guidance to apprentices, and set examinations with the help of 120,000 experts from industry that provide their services free of charge. Every year the chambers award half a million certificates to apprentices in 380 trades. The chambers also have a say in the content of training courses trying to ensure that courses meet practical needs, and are involved in the formulation of job profiles, which constantly need to be adapted to new requirements. Various seminars and courses are also provided for the instructors themselves.

Representation of interest groups and policy advice

Businesses benefit in particular from information and advice from their local chambers with regard to legislation. The chambers play the role of intermediary between business and Government. They act as a spokesperson for the business community *vis-à-vis* the political arena. Nearly every law that is passed affects the world of business in some way. The chambers therefore comment on bills in the drafting stage to ensure that business interests receive proper consideration. The advice and information which companies receive from the chambers gives them an early insight into political trends, statutory rulings and forthcoming legislation, to allow them to respond in good time to changed conditions and circumstances.

At local and district levels, the chambers will, for instance, comment on budget estimates or urban and regional plans. Here they are often involved in the detailed work of, say, road and railway planning or even public transport timetables.

At the State level, the chambers seek to maintain close contacts with the Government and its various departments, either by acting in a concerted manner or with one chamber acting on behalf of several others. The chambers of industry and commerce participate e.g. in development plans, business promotion schemes, education, taxation, and transport planning.

The Association of German Chambers of Industry and Commerce (DIHT), the chambers' central organization, looks after the business community's interests in respect of the federal Government, as well as with regard to the international arena. Its president speaks on behalf of all firms in all sectors of the economy and is elected for a four-year term by the annual general meeting of the chambers of industry and commerce. The DIHT has more than 200 staff, headed by an executive director. It is a registered association with headquarters at the seat of Government. Its responsibilities are laid down in its statutes. The DIHT is heard on all bills that affect industry. It advises federal Government, parliament and Government agencies. The DIHT also engages in dialog with the European Commission, the European Parliament and various international bodies, sometimes in cooperation with its counterpart organizations throughout Europe.

Selected service and consulting examples

Public-sector contracts

Germany's public sector spends around DM 400 million a year through public procurement. Since taxpayers finance these projects, they are also subject to special procedures and controls. The public sector is a customer like any other, albeit one with special purchasing rules. It is important for industry to know the rules that govern the award of public contracts and how they are applied. Businesses can only be suppliers to the public sector if they are suitably qualified. In some cases, proof of such qualification can be company or contract specific. There are three types of contract awards: public invitations to tender; limited invitations to tender; and discretionary contract awards.

The chambers of industry and commerce play a crucial role in limited invitations to tender. This method allows public bodies to approach a restricted number of companies and request them to submit tenders. The choice of companies for the shortlist to participate in a tender for public procurement is made by the chambers of industry and commerce. Public-sector customers pass their inquiries to a chamber, which then searches through its electronic databases for companies suitable as suppliers. The chamber then investigates whether these companies would indeed be willing and able to handle and complete the order. The names of those companies that fit

the tender are given to the customer, who then forwards the tender documentation to this limited group of suppliers.

In 1999, for example, the chamber of industry and commerce for the Stuttgart region alone processed around 1,600 invitations to tender in this way, passing on the names of 1,200 companies from the Stuttgart region. This clearly illustrates the important role of the chambers in mediating the award of public contracts: naming suitable suppliers to the various public-sector customers; and paving the way to business relationships between component suppliers and large corporations. The chambers' activities also include advice to companies, assisting them in acquiring public contracts, and supplying them with specific information about nationwide and EU-wide invitations to tender. This service is provided free of charge to members of the chamber of industry and commerce.

Electronic commerce

The chambers of industry and commerce have established a nationwide network to offer consulting on electronic business issues and the Internet to small and medium-sized businesses. Companies can approach the chambers with questions about, for example, setting up online shops, creating home pages, electronic payment systems, Internet connectivity, teleworking etc. To meet this need for advice and counselling, the chambers offer a combination of information events, publications, seminars, and workshops. On request, SMEs can also receive an initial introduction to the subject matter in the context of corporate consulting. For instance, the chamber of industry and commerce in Stuttgart provides this kind of advice to about 700 firms over the phone and to around 200 companies on site every year. The services on offer include advice on electronic business transactions and the Internet, how to present model solutions, assistance with Internet guides and checklists, and overviews of products and service providers.

The chamber has also set up working groups to allow businesses to share their experience and discuss problems. Workgroups dealing with Internet law, telecommunications and information technology are, for example, already in existence.

Advice on innovation

The chambers of industry and commerce have created a series of innovation and technology consulting centres. The advice on innovation is not "specialist consulting" but it rather helps companies to help themselves by supplying them with information about the state of the art, about industrial property rights and about the market; by putting them in touch with external experts in the scientific and business communities and by informing them about State subsidies and assistance for research and development.

The staff of the chambers of industry and commerce start by analysing a company's problems on site, working with the company to examine the following aspects: technical expertise; knowledge of the market; automation; system delivery; diversification; finance; environment problems; and waste disposal. The companies that use these services particularly appreciate the fact that the chambers offer this advice free of charge and in a neutral capacity. The portfolio of consulting and information services also includes support for the development of new products and processes; procuring information about the state of the art; advising companies with regard to patents and licenses; bringing them into contact with university developments and dissertations that are ready to be transferred; setting up links to venture capital resources through an investment exchange; and notifying firms of public subsidy programmes for research and development.

The chambers also exert an influence on technology policy. The chambers of industry and commerce seek to ensure that the Government's technology policy fosters a climate that is conducive to innovation, that creates and sustains an efficient structure for basic and applied research, and that gives due consideration to the needs of small and medium-sized enterprises.

Advice to start-ups

The chambers of industry and commerce offer a broad spectrum of information and consulting modules for people who are seeking to start up a business. The list that follows is merely a selection of the topics on which advice is available to would-be entrepreneurs:
- Personnel requirements
- company planning
- registering as a business
- issues relating to markets and locations
- legal forms and company names
- taxes
- social insurance contributions
- accounting responsibilities
- finance
- capital requirements
- subsidies.

Again taking the Stuttgart region as an example, more than 10,000 potential new entrepreneurs in the vicinity have taken advantage of the local chamber's information and consulting services. Over 21 staff representing a wide variety of disciplines have, for instance, been available to answer the questions of prospective entrepreneurs on legal and fiscal matters, marketing and finance.

Start-up consulting is one area where the chambers of industry and commerce really come into their own as a "one-stop agency". The network built up by the chambers offers information and advice on virtually every aspect of launching a new business. This is the only way to ensure that high-quality advice and information can be provided to entrepreneurs in every conceivable industry.

Foreign trade

A wide range and assortment of events and campaigns, the strong network that links the individual chambers throughout Germany, close cooperation with Germany's chambers of foreign trade and commerce and with other organizations all combine to enable the chambers to provide extremely efficient support to those companies in Germany that are oriented towards foreign trade. Businesses can draw on a very extensive range of information, advisory and other services:

➢ information and advice about countries and markets
➢ information about foreign business law
➢ advice on foreign direct investment
➢ information about German foreign trading legislation
➢ export controls and embargoes
➢ provision of contacts and addresses to initiate business relationships abroad information about foreign trade shows
➢ advice on how to handle export and import business
➢ the issue of carnets and certificates of origin
➢ the certification of commercial invoices and other transhipment documents.

Extensive continued training

The chambers organize tens of thousands of seminars and training courses. Every year 80,000 people who have received training organized by the chambers are awarded a certificate to this effect. Thus, electricians, for instance, can become master craftsmen in industry, cooks can become master chefs, and office clerks can move up the ladder of seniority. Further training and development courses are available for skilled craftsmen from all industries and all sizes of company.

Continued training and development covers such a wide range of possibilities that they all have to be stored in a database. Known by its German acronym of WIS, the Further Training and Development Information System helps companies find those courses that are best suited to their employees. The WIS provides access to 40,000 courses and a large number of instructors. The chambers also hold nearly a million individual discussions a year with employees and companies with a view to improving training.

Furthermore, the chambers abroad help German firms with local operations to provide apprenticeships and further training for their employees, too.

Information

The chambers advise companies on such matters as tax and finance, innovation, trade, and the environment. Corresponding databases offer a fast and reliable source of information. Some of these databases are published on the Internet and are in the public domain; most can be used at no charge (e.g. www.stuttgart.ihk.de and www.diht.de).

The chambers publish 79 magazines with a total circulation of 2.5 million. They keep companies informed on all major changes in company and tax law, the economic situation, trade, transport, apprenticeship and further training, energy, and environmental matters. In addition, nearly all chambers issue specialized brochures and maintain business libraries.

The chambers collate and evaluate domestic and foreign business statistics, but they also collect data of their own. Of particular interest are the spring and autumn economic surveys conducted by the DIHT, as these are based on first-hand information. Twenty-five thousand German companies reply to chamber questionnaires about their business prospects.

Summary

Compulsory membership for all industrial, retail and service companies puts Germany's chambers of industry and commerce right at the forefront of real-world business. The chambers are not dependent on public funding, so companies value the neutrality of the advice and information they provide. Moreover, the general assembly gives the entrepreneurs themselves a say in monitoring and controlling the service and consulting portfolio offered by the chambers. Their own experience thus helps the chambers to adapt their offerings quickly and flexibly to an ever-changing business climate.

Acceptance of these business advisory and information services hinges on whether the customers are ultimately satisfied. To examine whether this is so, independent market and sales research companies are commissioned to assess a representative random sample of these companies. In 1996, a nationwide representative survey found that 65 per cent were either satisfied or very satisfied with the performance of the chambers. Twenty per cent gave an average score, while 16 per cent were not satisfied. In this result, it is important to note that the chambers achieved higher marks among those companies that made more frequent use of their advisory and other services. The most recent analysis, conducted in 1999, revealed that 88 per cent of respondent companies were positive about their experience of information, consulting and services provided by the chambers of industry and commerce. Only 12 per cent reported negative experiences. In particular, the companies surveyed rated the technical expertise of the chambers' staff as good to very good.

The chambers refuse to rest on their laurels, however. At present, a uniform IT structure is being created nationwide to enable streamlined and comparable workflows to be put in place at each individual regional chamber. At the same time, the chambers of industry and commerce throughout Germany are just completing an exhaustive comparison with a view to harmonizing the costs, services and offerings available across the individual chambers. Existing resources of in-depth expertise are being concentrated better still and collated in an advanced knowledge management system. Competence centres are to be set up for specific areas of exceptional importance and will make their services available to the other chambers.

Outlook

The chambers of industry and commerce play a key role in the tightly meshed, nationwide network of economic development, business information and business consulting services in Germany. Their services are networked together with publicly funded offerings made available by the federal States, regional economic development departments, and district and municipal authorities. In the future it will be imperative to ensure that economic development is organized with constancy, transparency, and based on a forward-looking mindset. Given the considerable number of organizations operating on different levels, closer cooperation between them is vital. In many cases, companies do not have a clear view of which organizations or institutions could best help them in a particular set of circumstances. In the Stuttgart region alone, for example, companies can choose between up to five different contact points. The objective in the future must be to coordinate the measures applied and press ahead with the use of modern means of communication. Improved networking is the only way to avoid duplicating efforts.

Hungary

There are seven EICs in the Hungarian Network. One of the main targets of the EICs in the period of EU enlargement is to help SMEs become competitive and prepare them for EU access.

The Hungarian EIC network has carried out a promotional campaign to familiarize SMEs with the benefits of using IT, quality systems and innovation. To this end, seminars and conferences were organized, and brochures and articles published on these topics. Through local, regional and national media and the Internet, 84,000 enterprises were contacted.

The Euro Info Centre in Szekszard was established at the Chamber of Commerce and Industry of Tolna County in 1999, when the EIC Network was enlarged to the central and eastern European countries. Working together with local, regional and national partners and using the opportunities of the EIC Network throughout

Europe, EIC Szekszard provides several services to SMEs, such as information on EU and national legislations and rules, standards and tenders and helps SMEs in searching for business cooperation partners.

Israel

National SME Strategy

SMEs are regarded as a key element in the Israeli economy, constituting 98% of the total number of enterprises in the country and accounting for 60% of all employees in the private sector.

Government policy is to encourage SMEs and potential entrepreneurs, assist them in overcoming the obstacles impeding their success, enhance their competitive capacity and expand their share in the economy through a variety of support programmes geared to the various segments of the Israeli population.

Support Agents

ISMEA – the Israel SMEs Authority is the main agent, which initiates and applies Government policies for encouraging SMEs.

These include the following activities :
➢ Creating and activating various means of supporting SMEs.
➢ Activating and coordinating all agencies and bodies functioning in the field of SMEs.
➢ Setting up local, regional and professional centres for encouraging SMEs; assisting, guiding and monitoring the activities of these centres (SBDCs), which include information and guidance services, counselling, training, tutoring and referrals to sources of funding.
➢ Conducting education and training in managing, establishing and operating SMEs.
➢ Initiating entrepreneurial education.

➢ Establishing data bases in the SMEs sector.
➢ Initiate the establishment of capital funds and other financial resources for SMEs.
➢ Creating supportive public opinion for SMEs.
➢ Operating preferential support programmes for specific target groups: SMEs in peripheral areas, in the Arab and Druze sector, new immigrants, women entrepreneurs and demobilized soldiers.
➢ Activating Support Centre (SBDC) for Technological Entrepreneurs.
➢ Operating Innovation Management Techniques Programmes.

Ministry of Industry and Trade Support Programmes:

➢ Business Tutoring Programme.
➢ State Guarantee Fund for Encouraging SMEs.
➢ Investment Centre.
➢ Marketing Promotion Fund.

Office of the Chief Scientist – Ministry of Industry and Trade

➢ Implements Government policy in support of R&D through "Law for Encouragement of Industrial R&D", which enhances development of technological industry by means of grants for development of new products, start-ups and projects in development areas.
➢ Implements the Technological Incubators Programme, which enables novice entrepreneurs with innovative concepts to translate them into commercial products.
➢ Implements the "Tnufa" Programme which assists technological inventors during the earliest stages of their products, evaluates their technological and commercial potential, extends legal advice, marketing consultancy and assistance in mobilizing capital.
➢ Implements the "Magnet" Programme, which supports R&D for generic pre-

competitive technologies (also for large enterprises).

The Israel Export Institute

The Institute implements a special programme for new and beginning exporters.

The Ministry of Absorption

The Ministry of Absorption implements a special SME support programme for new immigrants within the framework of the SBDCs (Small Business Development Centres) operated by ISMEA. The programme includes consultancy services, training courses and seminars geared to the needs of new immigrants.

The Absorption Ministry has also established a special Fund for New Immigrants, which grants subsidized loans at very convenient terms.

The above agents cover a comprehensive support framework for SMEs in all sectors of the economy which implements the Government's policy to extend all the assistance required by SMEs in order to expand the part they play in the Israeli economy.

Poland

On 27 October 1998, the Council of Ministers approved the Business Activity Law bill. The main rationale behind the bill was to impose an obligation on public administration authorities to create conditions fostering the operation and development of small and medium-sized enterprises.

On 11 May, 1999, the Council of Ministers approved the "Government SME Action Framework until 2002". The document specifies how the obligations arising under the Business Activity Law should be met. The main aims of the Law include:

➢ improving the competitiveness of small and medium-sized enterprises
➢ increasing SME exports
➢ expanding capital investment expenditures in the SME sector.

The Department of Crafts and SMEs at the Ministry of the Economy is responsible for policy-making issues in relation to small and medium-sized enterprises.

In June 1999, the Regional Policy and Balanced Development Committee of the Council of Ministers approved a concept for the National Strategy of Regional Development 2000–2006. The principal SME support instruments include:
➢ start-up subsidies increasing the level of capital investment, particularly for those SMEs based on modern technologies or supporting the environment;
➢ subsidies for regional investment, credit and loan guarantee funds targeted at SMEs;
➢ partial financing of SME advisory services provided by specialist business support organizations;
➢ business incubators, local and regional development agencies.

In 1999, SME-focused government action was noticeably stepped up. This is undoubtedly the result of Poland's EU accession process, but also demonstrates the growing importance of the SME sector in Poland. Under the Regulation of the Council of Ministers, on 13 June 2000, the Ministry of Regional Development and Construction was set up. As part of its regional development remit, the Regional Development Programming Department and Voivodship Relations and Assistance Programmes Department were established.

Government policy on small and medium-sized enterprises is directed at the following:
➢ to create adequate conditions for their establishment and development
➢ to increase opportunities for development
➢ to provide wider access to training and information

> to create conditions which will help to increase the competitiveness of products and services offered by small and medium-sized enterprises on national and international markets.

SME Support Institutions

Business support organizations improve the environment in which small and medium-sized enterprises operate. They include both non-profit organizations and purely profit-driven ventures.

There are four groups of such organizations:
> entities providing services to SMEs
> entrepreneur organizations
> NGOs focused on SMEs
> research institutes and academic units.

In 1999, a total of 1,508 SME support organizations were registered. Most of the business support providers were set up in 1991–1994. In terms of the support agenda, the most frequent service offered to SMEs is training. Advisory and information services are also quite popular. Certification and standardization services are those least frequently placed on activity lists.

In general terms, it can be said that uncomplicated services are the ones that entrepreneurs use most frequently. Specialist industry-specific services are still underused, despite the fact that the beneficiaries of advisory services are already existing companies, rather than start-ups .

Polish Agency for Enterprise Development

The Agency for Enterprise Development is a government agency established in 2001 as the result of the transformation of the Polish Foundation for Small and Medium Enterprise Promotion and Development, which had been active in the years of 1996-2000. It is subordinate to the Minister of the Economy. The objectives of the Agency include implementation of economic development in programmes, especially in the areas of:
> Development of small and medium-sized enterprises (SMEs)
> Exports
> Social and economic cohesion.

These objectives are pursued, among other means, through:
> Provision of consultancy and expert services to entrepreneurs and to government and municipal administrations
> Facilitation of access by entrepreneurs to knowledge, training, economic information, and financing
> Information provision and promotion.

National SME Services Network (KSU)

During the five years of operation of the Polish Foundation for Small and Medium Enterprise Promotion and Development, an organizational infrastructure for supporting the development of the SME sector in Poland was established. This is the National SME Services Network, a group of some 150 cooperating business counselling centres around the country. Most of the member organizations are regional and local development agencies, business support centres, industrial and commercial chambers, and local foundations and associations; all of them are not-for-profit entities providing services directly to SMEs. These entities operate under an accreditation system that guarantees maintenance of high standards in their advisory, training, information and financial services. Since 2000, the National SME Network centres have been participating in the implementation of the Government's policy regarding small and medium-size enterprises. The year 2001 will see continued development of the system as an instrument for consolidating non-profit organizations working to the benefit of SMEs and for improving the quality of their services.

Polish Regional Development Foundations

The mission of the Polish Regional Development Foundations is to support the development of SMEs, and in doing so, to support the local economy and to promote their regions both domestically and internationally. To create an environment conducive to enterprise development, its instruments include advisory and consulting services, training as well as guarantees for loans. The foundations develop networks of SME support organizations in the country.

Business Support Units

Business support units are, alongside organizations for entrepreneurs, a very significant component of the business support environment. They are non-profit organizations that specialize in providing advisory, information and training services to small and medium-sized enterprises or individuals starting a business.

Business support units comprise:
➤ Business Support Centres (BSCs), the main aims of which include:
  - advisory services for SME fine-tuned to the requirements of individual enterprise development stages, covering the general scope of knowledge about running a business as well as business management, finances, technology and processes, marketing, production;
  - training for SMEs complementing the market offer, targeting the needs of a sector, categories of enterprises or tailor-made;
  - provision of business information and facilitating business relations relying on the existing networks and international, national and regional sources.
➤ In addition, BSCs engage in activities aimed at creating a good environment that fosters enterprise in a given region, among others by participation in regional development programmes and strategies and disseminating information on the role and situation in the SME sector.
➤ Business Information Centres, which specialize in the provision of information

on running a business to small and medium-sized enterprises and other customers. Most often, these are not stand-alone entities but subsidiary units of other business support organizations.
➤ Business Incubators where the environment created is to satisfy the needs of enterprises in the most crucial stage of their development. An incubator helps enterprises survive by providing them with all types of specialist advice, facilitating access to sources of funds, offering joint premises in which to conduct business or ensuring office and administrative back-up.
➤ Innovation and Technology Centres, which specialize in the provision of services relating to innovation and technology transfer to enterprises by, for instance, offering information on research programmes, technology development and innovation projects in the EU; promotional activities; training; advice or technology transfer financing.
➤ Research Centres that are most often units of larger organizations, which provide services to SMEs (they will be discussed at length in due course), while agricultural extension centres are most often stand-alone entities.
➤ Non-profit Financial Institutions that are most often grant, subsidy, loan and loan guarantee funds operating as separate units of larger SME support organizations.

Organizations of Entrepreneurs

In 1999, the total of 566 organizations whose members were entrepreneurs were registered. Entrepreneurs can set up their own organizations in accordance with the following acts of law:
➤ Act of 22 March 1989 on Crafts (Dz. U. No. 17, item 92);
➤ Act of 30 May 1989 on Chambers of Commerce (Dz. U. No. 35, item 195);
➤ Act of 30 May 1989 on Professional Self-Regulation of Certain Business Entities (Dz. U. No. 17, item 194);

- Act of 23 May 1991 on Employer Organizations (Dz. U. No. 55, item 235);
- Law of Associations (Dz. U. 1989 no. 20, item 104, amended in 1990 no. 14, item 86).

The operations of entrepreneur organizations are not limited to furthering the interests of their members, they also engage in a variety of activities constituting an important component of the business environment. While during recent years the popularity of information and advisory services has slightly weakened, training continues to be much in demand. Strangely enough, the popularity of lobbying, which should be a natural type of activity for this type of organization, remains relatively small.

Non-Governmental Organizations Supporting SMEs

Regional and local development agencies are the most frequent type of non-Governmental organizations providing services to SMEs. The agencies existing currently in Poland do not operate based on any uniform legal framework. The for-profit agencies most often take the legal form of a joint-stock or limited liability company. Non-profit organizations operate as foundations, joint-stock companies or associations. None of the legal forms available to choose from in Poland meets the specific requirements of a local or regional development agency, either for legal reasons (companies) or because of difficulties stemming from the practices of the courts or tax offices (foundations).

The main functions of the agencies include:
- fostering economic development by creating and implementing regional restructuring programmes (restructuring programme development, conducting reorganization and liquidation processes, equity investment in privatization processes, based on the agency's funds);
- supporting measures to counteract unemployment (vocational training, skills improvement, job clubs stimulating the unemployed in their job seeking efforts, information centres providing information on the requirements of the labour market, job exchanges);
- harmonizing economic and social development;
  - assistance in the establishment of and support for educational, information and advisory infrastructure for small and medium-sized enterprises. These tasks are usually undertaken by the separate units, discussed above (business support centres, business incubators, information centres, etc.);
  - assistance to SMEs in gaining access to external sources of funds. The tools used include loan guarantee funds, which provide guarantees to SMEs as security for credit facilities procured by them from banks. Mutual guarantee funds are a special category here. Apart from loan guarantee funds, venture capital funds are the most frequently used tool in providing assistance to SMEs aimed at facilitating access to capital;
  - support for innovation and cooperation between research centres, and the economy and administration (fostering local inventions, developing programmes of cooperation between research and academic institutions and business organizations);
- regional promotion (promotion of inward investment and regional geographic location strengths, promotion of regional products and services, etc.).

National System of SME Services

The National System of SME Services (NSSS) was set up in 1996 on the initiative of the Polish Foundation for SME Promotion. NSSS is aimed at developing a comprehensive service market targeted at SMEs, based on local, regional and national enterprise support organizations.

There are some 130 non-profit and for-profit organizations operating within NSSS. All these organizations are engaged in the provision of advisory, training, information, financial and industry-specific services to SMEs.

Commercial Consulting and Advisory Business Situation in Poland

In 1999, small consulting companies fought to attract the attention of customers to their service offering in market niches, such as external communications and IT support. Owing to the relatively sluggish economic growth in 2000, many companies experienced a shrinking market for consulting services. It can be argued that the reason was that too few privatization programmes were implemented, and the Polish consulting companies work above all for the Minister of State Treasury, in conducting studies and developing enterprise sale programmes. Polish consulting companies are starting to concentrate on restructuring and support programmes for Polish enterprises to help them realign with the EU standards.

Business Information Network (BIN)

The network consists of 24 business information centres whose scope of operation covers all of Poland. The objective of the centres is to support small and medium-sized enterprises in Poland by providing the information required to start and grow a business. The BIN network operates the Entrepreneur's Guide database that holds over 350 different information packages divided into 26 leading topic categories.

The European Commission's programme BC–NET (Business Cooperation Network) is an information system targeted at small and medium-sized enterprises, offering business opportunities information (trade, financial and technical). The aim of BC-NET is to foster international business relations between SMEs and provides assistance in finding business partners abroad by distributing cooperation requests. The BC–NET in Poland comprises 12 accredited facilities. The Polish SME Foundation is the National Contact Centre.

The National SME Service Network (KSU) is an example of a network which integrates institutions supporting SMEs. The network consists of SME support institutions and institutions which promote development of services for this sector.

It was established in 1996 as a result of the initiative of the Polish Foundation for the Promotion and Development of Small and Medium-sized Enterprises. The aim of the Network is to develop a broad market of services for SMEs based on local, regional and national institutions supporting entrepreneurship.

Centres within the network cooperate to:
➢ Exchange information and ensure cooperation between network members, which should stimulate improvement of the scope and quality of services rendered and mutual use of the potential and resources, which should make it possible to avoid repetition and duplication of activities;
➢ Correlate activities of the network of business environment institutions with the economic and social policy of the State;
➢ Exchange information, knowledge, resources and products, and as a result of that to increase the range of services offered by the centres.

In 1999 the network consisted of 130 local and regional business support centres, which have been providing consulting, training, information, financial and other special services for the SME sector.

Each centre in the network has its own specialization and operates in a specific region. The cooperation between them makes it possible to draw on the offer of another organization in cases when the one approached by a potential client does not specialize in the requested services. The exchange of experience improves the qualifications of each centre's staff. As a result of this, entrepreneurs are able to receive easy-to-access and high quality services.

Below, some agencies providing business advisory, counselling and information services in Poland are described as examples.

Konin Regional Development Agency (RDA)

The Konin Regional Development Agency (RDA) was established in 1992 as an institution for the support of restructuring and economic development in the Konin province (currently Wielkopolska).

Advisory services for SMEs in the Konin RDA begun in 1994, when a PHARE private sector development programme decided to create a business support organization (BSO) in the agency. The programme started business support activities with partial financing for two years. After organizing an infrastructure for business support with personnel, knowledge, equipment, etc., the agency concentrated on the development of skills and markets.

In 1994, the BSO started to deliver simple advisory and information services for start-ups. This activity is still going on and in addition, as part of its own development, the Konin BSO now also offers services to existing companies as well as to start-ups. At the beginning, the BSO cooperated with small, new enterprises, but consequently developed skills and accumulated experience that have led to another market – companies with 20 – 50 employees.

From 1996 the Konin RDA has systematically improved its advisory methods for SMEs based on cooperation with Polish and foreign consultants dispatched through different programmes Many times the RDA has worked as a junior consultant, learning by doing with senior experts in services for SMEs. The key elements in this process were:
- ➢ cooperation with the Polish SME Foundation and the KSU
- ➢ USAID project "FIRMA 2000"
- ➢ Project on "Masterplan Development of the Konin Province to 2010"

Cooperation with the Polish SME Agency and membership in the KSU play the most important role for the business support activities at the Konin RDA. From 1997 the Konin RDA has participated in more than 20 different SME projects delivering advisory, training and information services, financed by the European Commission and the Government of Poland.

Cooperation with American and Japanese experts has had an especially important role in the development of the Konin RDA as a professional business support organization.

In 1997 USAID started a business support project "FIRMA 2000". It delivered advanced advisory methodologies through direct cooperation between Polish and American advisors working in small and medium-sized companies. There were two important areas of interest of the project:
- ➢ development of professional advisory services delivered by a BSO
- ➢ direct advisory and training for SMEs in the area of management, marketing and finance.

During these three years the Konin RDA employees attended training and workshops and individual consultations increasing the capabilities of the advisory services of the BSO.

The project helped the RDA to prepare a Market Segmentation and Service Portfolio as well as its own Capability Statement and Development Strategy. The RDA organized numerous advisory consultations and training services with United States experts in marketing, management and finance.

As a result of the three years of cooperation the Konin RDA:

- ➢ increased its own management effectiveness
- ➢ increased the qualifications of its advisors
- ➢ developed knowledge in management, marketing and finance

- developed markets
- increased the market identification of the RDA.

During the same period the Japanese operated a project in the province a project on the Masterplan for Regional Development of the Konin Province to 2010. In the main project, the Konin RDA participated in the market research on SMEs, which delivered a wealth of information about the SME sector in the province and allowed an understanding of the different types of requirements of SMEs. Thanks to the advisors, the RDA also familiarized itself with the Japanese methodology of advisory management, marketing and Total Quality Management (TQM) and the Kaizen approach in particular.

Thanks to these priority projects, the RDA gained a position where it can now play an important role in regional development policy, as a professional institution supporting SMEs in:

- re-education of managers in management and production technology
- diffusion of TQM and Kaizen
- travel services for SMEs.

Since 1997 the RDA has consequently built its regional position in advisory, training and information services. During these three years the RDA has delivered hundreds of advisory consultations and information services and trained thousands of managers and employees in management, marketing and finance. The main areas of its competence are:

- advisory services for development strategies, business plans, restructuring plans, market research
- marketing strategies
- training in strategic management, human resources management, marketing and finance.

The development of advisory and training services for SMEs is connected on the one hand with permanent cooperation with Polish and foreign trainers and advisors and, on the other hand, with continued in-house development. In 1999, the province became part of Wielkopolska Province – a region with 3 million inhabitants and around 150,000 SMEs. Since 1998 already, the Konin Regional Development Agency has been preparing plans for support systems for SMEs in Wielkopolska. In 1999 the RDA started to organize training and advisory services in different places in Wielkopolska, mostly concentrated on the territory of the former Konin Province and actively participated and worked in the process of creating a development strategy for Wielkopolska Province.

In June 2000 Wielkopolska Province finished a development strategy where the development of SMEs plays an important role in assuring the competitiveness of the region. There are four operational goals identified in the development strategy connected to SME sector development :

- increase in the competitiveness of SMEs
- creation of jobs
- increase in the export capabilities of SMEs
- restructuring of some branches, such as food processing.

"Free Entrepreneurship" Association, Gdańsk

The "Free Entrepreneurship" Association and its regional branch in Gdańsk provides consulting and training services to small and medium-sized private businesses in the Pomeranian region in Poland. The mission of the Association is to help entrepreneurs establish and develop businesses with a strong long-term competitive edge. It implements advisory projects for small and medium-sized enterprises (SMEs) within European Union assistance programmes.

Consulting Services

The Association offers advisory services on:
- taxes
- finance (completing loan applications and business plans)
- marketing
- law

- management information systems
- human resources management.

Entrepreneurs may take advantage of complex advisory services offered by the Association's experts. During the first, free of charge meeting with a client the consultant identifies the most vital problems of the client's business. Sometimes consultants suggest solutions to these problems right away but more often they establish a longer term cooperation with the client company. It allows them to analyse the problems in different areas of a business operation in more detail. As a consequence of that analysis the consultants present to the client a plan with specific actions and undertakings within a new, consistent and more effective strategy.

Training and Seminars

Training programmes are addressed to people who would like to become or already are entrepreneurs. Training covers a wide range of topics in the area of marketing, sales techniques, taxes, management, TQM and human resources management as well as referring to other current issues important to SMEs. An excellent example of the latter may be a series of courses about the requirements for SMEs that would like to participate in the Highway Construction Programme.

Seminars aimed at providing entrepreneurs with information on specific topics are also organized. Specialists and experts in different business areas conduct these seminars. Recently Polish entrepreneurs have become especially interested in the seminars on European law and legal requirements for Polish SMEs willing to operate in the European Union market.

Business Information

The Euro Info Centre and Business Information Centre in Gdańsk, operating within the Association, specialize in business information services. The centres use information resources such as: data bases of Polish and foreign companies looking for business partners, databases containing legal documents of Poland and the European Union, the Internet, a library of official European Commission publications, books and magazines discussing issues related to the European integration process.

The following business information is provided:
o contact information (address, telephone number, etc.) to a specific company or group of companies from a specific region, country or continent
o legal and economic regulations in the European Union countries
o European Union assistance programmes for Polish SMEs
o search for business partners in and outside of Poland
o Check of business partners' credibility (company commercial reports)
o market analyses
o consulting on how to create management information systems

The association has represented Polish SMEs in business negotiations with entrepreneurs from France, Norway, Spain, Sweden and Ukraine. The Association belongs to the National System of Services for SMEs and Business Information Network. It also cooperates with the Polish Association of Women Entrepreneurs.

The Regional Branch in Gdańsk consists of the six following local offices in the Pomeranian region:
- Business Support Centre in Gdynia, operating since 1992
- Business Support Centre in Kartuzy, operating since 1993
- Business Support Centre Centrum in Lębork, operating since 1993
- Euro Info Centre in Gdańsk, operating since 1994
- Business Information Centre in Gdańsk, operating since 1994
- Gdańsk Advisory and Training Centre, operating since 1995.

Networking among Business Services Institutions

Networking is a method of improving the efficiency of Business Services Organizations. Here are three examples of Business Support Networks in Poland:

The Business Information Network (BIN) consists of 22 information centres operating all over Poland. They support small and medium-sized enterprises providing information necessary to establish and develop a business. The Network offers the Entrepreneur Guide database, which contains more than 350 information packets grouped into 26 divisions, such as banking and

Euro Info Centres (EIC)

The network of 12 Euro Info Centres was established in Poland in 1999. The Centres inform, advise and assist small and medium-sized enterprises all over Poland. They give answers to business questions, organize seminars, publish bulletins and business guides, provide enterprises with information and advice on European regulations, public procurement, European programmes and financing or partners search.

Lublin Development Foundation

Lublin Development Foundation (Lubelska Fundacja Rozwoju) (LDF) was set up in September 1991 on the initiative of local institutions and organizations, which perceived the economic development of the Lublin region as a top priority. At that time, the financial resources of LDF amounted to USD 100,000; today its capital totals USD 5,000,000. LDF is a Regional Development Agency operating in the Lublin region.

Over the period of its operations, LDF emerged as a leader in supporting small and medium-sized enterprises. It is perceived as one of the most significant organizations supporting regional restructuring initiatives. It is seen as a modern and reliable company supporting SMEs and a reputable financial institution specializing

also in providing advisory and training services. As the findings of audit exercises demonstrate, the services offered by the Lublin Development Foundation mean professionalism and quality. The numerous projects and initiatives undertaken by the individual programme units specializing in specific areas have also contributed to enhancing the image of the Foundation.

The mission of the Lublin Development Foundation is to:
➤ support the development of small and medium-sized enterprises in the Lublin region
➤ support the local economy's restructuring process
➤ promote the region at home and abroad
➤ create an environment conducive to enterprise development.

This work is carried out through:
➤ Promoting the region and the local economy
➤ Advisory and consulting services
➤ Training services
➤ Developing a network of SME support organizations:
  - Regional Development Agencies
  - Business Support Centres
  - Business incubators
➤ Execution, administration and management of assistance programmes
➤ Info Centre
➤ Loan guarantee service
➤ Guarantee service for loan advances from the Employment Office
➤ Extending loans
➤ Business financing through equity investment.

Advisory and Consulting Services

The Consulting Division of the Lublin Development Foundation offers a wide range of basic and advanced professional advisory services intended for enterprises regardless of their size and scale of operation and for local officials involved in the management of local budgets (town and municipality/locality).

The advisory and consulting services are tailored to meet the requirements of each group of SME customers, including established entrepreneurs, start-ups and individuals planning to become self-employed.

Advanced Advisory and Consulting Services

Experience shows that enterprises operating for many years in business use these services most often. In order to live up to the expectations of our customers we offer the following advisory services:

➤ Financial consulting: a comprehensive, specialist financial service supplying the best possible solutions in such areas as: privatization, business health-check and diagnosis, financial projects and studies, risk management.

➤ Financial projects: are those that entrepreneurs find most appealing, regardless of the standing of the enterprise. Often companies request a consultant's assistance in prospecting for an external investor; in most cases however these enterprises are in a pretty good shape. Currently, most likely due to the deterioration of the situation of SMEs in Poland, companies which require restructuring at different levels of their business turn to us for assistance, often at the request of the financing institution (bank), but also without any external stimulus, becoming acutely aware of difficulties in surviving in the market. The level of education and the period of operation of the entrepreneur is not important here, the prime driving force is the need for an external, objective assessment.

➤ Organizational and legal advice: assistance in organising the enterprise, negotiations and acquisition/transfer of shares, establishment of joint-venture businesses, developing specialist assessments.

➤ Marketing advice: market research, marketing and promotional strategy development, marketing and sales department rationalization proposals, sales support strategy planning and implementation, PR consulting.

➤ Management consulting: assistance in the organization of the enterprise and management systems, delineating functional responsibilities in the organizational structure and personnel management.

➤ Quality systems consulting: implementation of an effective ISO 9000-compliant Quality Assurance System; management and staff training; internal auditor training; assistance in the implementation of the Quality Manual, Procedures and Instructions; overseeing the implementation process; conducting a complete set of audits; assistance in selecting the certification company.

A team of LDF-accredited consultants includes at the moment several dozen of specialists with many years' experience in working with Polish and foreign companies. The accreditation system in place enables the engagement of independent consultants or advisors employed by other consulting companies as well as setting up interdisciplinary task forces dedicated to each of the projects. Small, medium-sized and large enterprises based in the Lublin region are the beneficiaries of the assistance provided by the Consulting Division.

Basic Advisory and Information Services

Given that individuals starting their own business and entrepreneurs that have been operating in the market for over a short period of time require information, the Consulting Division of the Lublin Development Foundation has also developed a special service package. It needs stressing that these services are usually provided free of charge (except when they require substantial time to be devoted by the consultant).

Advisory and information service offering:

➤ The so-called Start–up Package: simple advisory and information services aimed at start-ups. Despite – in our opinion – the quite straightforward procedure for dealing with the formalities on starting up a business or conducting a business at an early stage, the start-up services have proved extremely popular. The Foundation staff do much more than just provide information, they offer advice; for example on choosing the best taxation option depending on the type of business, on accounting, they also match business partners (e.g. a person who has commercial premises to let and a person who is looking for such premises). It is impossible to cover all the activities that go into the start–up package; they are always tailored to the type of undertaking proposed and the level of knowledge that the beneficiary already has.

➤ Information on the day-to-day running and management of a business.

➤ Information on external financing options available to SMEs.

➤ Regular cooperation with all the local SME financing institutions, as well as detailed and always up-to-date knowledge of their offering helps LDF staff to provide advice on selecting the best for a given external financing options (banks, leasing companies, guarantee funds, loan funds, venture capital funds).

➤ Information on assistance programmes available to SMEs.

➤ Information on more sophisticated consulting service offerings – including those partly financed by the EU and the Ministry of the Economy.

➤ While the awareness of individuals trying to go it alone in business has greatly improved over the recent years, it is still not sufficient. Only infrequently do entrepreneurs perceive a business plan as the key success factor in a given undertaking. The trial and error approach dominates – entrepreneurs are more likely to pin their hopes on luck than on the application of professional business methods. The staff of LDF always encourage their customers to conduct a detailed analysis of the proposed business project to help them evaluate its success probability.

➤ As from June 2001 the services provided by the Advisory and Consulting Centre are financed by the Ministry of the Economy.

Training Services

The basic aim of these services is to provide training to management teams of enterprises and local government officials, improving the vocational skills of the unemployed and prepare young people for their labour market entry.

The Training Centre offers the following types of training: basics of running a business, legal acts governing business activity, accounting, finance, marketing, management, human resources management, management skills, ISO 9000, computer operating skills.

Training sessions, delivered in training rooms with professional equipment to groups of 10–15 students, combine discussion, exercises and practical problem solving. The main focus of any training activity is on practical skills improvement, by pointing to modern and proven solutions. In addition, customized training is also run under contracts with specific companies, aligned with customers' industry-specific needs, delivered either on the company premises or in a selected training facility. The customers are actively engaged in developing tailor-made training programmes, whenever necessary, drawing on the experience of LDF-accredited consultants.

Development of an SME Support Network

Currently, the Local Development Agency network consists of seven local outposts, which are inseparably linked with the Lublin

Development Foundation and pursue the mission of LDF all over the Lublin region. The establishment of an LDA is always the result of a local initiative (town authorities, entrepreneurs). As a rule, town authorities provide a facility for the establishment of an LDA and the Lublin Development Foundation upgrades it. The specific operations undertaken by each of these LDAs are strictly adapted to the needs of the local community. The staff of the Agency, through their everyday contacts with local entrepreneurs and knowledge of their problems, can develop increasingly effective assistance proposals. The immediate availability of the Agency close at hand is also an important factor for entrepreneurs.

The basic activities that LDAs engage in include:
> Job Club – labour market counselling
> Employment services (licensed by the National Employment Office)
> Cooperation with other institutions (District Employment Office, City and Municipality Office, Local Traders' and Entrepreneurs' Associations, Foundations and support organizations, Municipal Social Assistance Centre, other local associations)
> Local promotion
> Advisory and information services related to the economic and legal aspects of doing business intended for existing SMEs and individuals setting up shop – Start-up Packages. Entrepreneurs are also advised of the more advanced advisory services delivered by LDF consultants and all other projects of the Foundation
> Training.

Thanks to professionally equipped training facilities, training is delivered on the premises of the Agency or on a complementary basis with the LDF's Training Centre in Lublin.

In an attempt to reach all interested parties with LDF's offering we have developed a network of Business Support Centres, whose scope of operation currently covers 8 towns. BSCs contribute to the achievement of the Foundation's mission by providing technical support to small and medium-sized enterprises, acting as intermediaries in exchanging business information, offering basic advisory services to SMEs and individuals who wish to become self-employed, providing assistance in preparing business plans and loan applications, maintaining a stock of reference books for entrepreneurs, and informing businesses and entrepreneurs of services and other current initiatives of the Lublin Development Foundation.

The Lublin Development Foundation also operates a business incubator. The total area available to entrepreneurs is in excess of 2,500 square metres. Currently the incubator has 30 tenant companies.

EIC was set up as part of the Euro Info Centres project initiated in 1986 by the European Commission. The operations of the Centre are partly financed by the Lublin Development Foundation and the Directorate General for Enterprise. The objective of EIC is to prepare small and medium-sized enterprises operating in the Lublin region for the integration of Poland with the EU.

The main tasks of EIC include the provision of information on the European Union, and in particular on: member countries, economic events, EU institutions, assistance programmes available to SMEs, business opportunities, European Commission events for the SME sector and the organization of economic events.

Bank Loan Guarantees

LDF's Loan Guarantee Fund (Lubelski Fundusz Przedsiębiorczości) provides loan guarantees to SMEs located in the Lublin region. The guarantee service has assisted many SMEs in gaining access to bank credit, helped increase bank lending as well as creating new jobs. At the moment, the resources available for the Fund's operations total over USD 2,000,000. The agreements made with banks provide for a multiplier effect of 3 to 1, which means that banks accept guarantees with an aggregate value equal to three times the amount of money available for that purpose.

Up to 70 per cent of a loan's principal is eligible for guarantee; however, not less than PLN 15,000 and not more than PLN 400,000. At the moment LGF works closely with 11 banks, extending loan guarantees to SMEs in the Lublin region representing all sectors of the economy, with the exception of defence, tobacco and distilling.

From 1995 to the end of June 2001 a total of 418 loan guarantees were extended for USD 7 million, with the value of related credit facilities amounting to USD 11 million. Thanks to its performance, the Fund was ranked first on the ranking list of regional and local loan guarantees in Poland. LGF has also a very low failure rate, a mere 0.4%.

Guarantees for Employment Office Loans

LDF's Local Guarantee Fund extends guarantees for loans advanced by the Employment Office. The service is targeted at individuals planning to start their own business and employers who are planning to create new jobs. The Local Guarantee Fund ensures easier access to loans advanced by the County Employment Office and, by so doing makes starting a business easier as well as helping to reduce unemployment in the Lublin region.

The extent of the guarantee cannot be higher than 70 per cent of the loan principal; also it cannot be lower than PLN 5,000 (some USD 1,140) or higher than PLN 20,000 (over USD 4,500).

Lending

LDF's Loan Fund grants loans to individuals intending to create new jobs, to the unemployed and those working under notice and intending to become self-employed. Some 22 counties of the Lublin region are expected to participate in the programme. The maximum loan

amount may not be higher than PLN 20,000 (over USD 4,500) and the repayment period is up to 18 months.

Equity Fund

LDF's Equity Investment Fund (Fundusz Kapitałowy) deals with financing business enterprises though equity investments and other debt instruments forming part of an integrated package. The EIF offering targets Lublin region SMEs, with the exception of those operating in the defence, tobacco and distilling industry. The minimum equity investment amount is USD 15,000, and the maximum USD 200,000 (equivalent in PLN at the current exchange rate). EIF is a local venture capital fund and as other funds of this type, by investing money in companies that are at a crucial growth stage in their development, alongside other owners, bears the inherent risk of the company doing business in the market economy. The effect of such an investment is the appreciation of the market value of portfolio companies. A telecom company can serve as a good illustration of this strategy: the value of the business increased after EIF's investment from some PLN 500,000 to PLN 10 million within just three years. Lubelski Fundusz Kapitałowy Sp. z o.o. is a passive investor and does not interfere with the day-to-day management of the company. However, during the period of the Fund's involvement, beneficiary companies can draw on the professional consulting services provided by EIF's staff and consultants.

From 1995 to the first half of this year, the Fund received and processed 377 equity investment applications. Its investment portfolio is comprised of 8 companies. The total value of equity investment todate is in excess of USD 1 million.

Business Support Organization in Podkarpackie Province

In 1999 some 70 organizations supporting SMEs were registered in the region, such as:

- ➤ chambers of commerce
- ➤ craft chambers
- ➤ business support entres
- ➤ associations
- ➤ regional development agencies
- ➤ foundation supporting SMEs.

The main objective for all these organizations is to provide support for small and medium-sized companies in our region in the field of education, management and development.

One of them is the Association of Entrepreneurship Promotion in Rzeszow, established in 1992 as an independent, non-Governmental, non-profit institution. Through its activity in the fields of education, advisory services, information technology, and industrial research, and due to various social and economic activities, provides professional assistance in the difficult process of industrial restructuring of south-eastern Poland.

Currently, the association is also witnessing fast growth in the range of information, advisory and educational services it offers to various organizations and companies from all over Poland. Additionally it carries out important contracts mandated directly by the European Union.

The main objective is to provide information and advisory services to small and medium-sized companies located mostly in Podkarpackie Province. The Association is deeply engaged in addressing the current problems of business enterprises: formulating solutions, and then monitoring and evaluating the process of their implementation.

The Association is divided into specific departments. The constant attention paid to the development of the Association attributes to its professionalism and the high level of offered services. Today, the association is one of the largest educational and advisory institutions in Poland. The graduates of our schools are highly appreciated in the job market.

Current undertakings

The Association of Entrepreneurship Promotion is the exclusive holder of the copyright on the COM STRAT game in Poland. COM STRAT is an original computer simulation elaborated by a team of Danish Technological Institute employees, which enables us to understand the functioning of the rules of the market. It is especially helpful in managing companies in which the hitherto existing management policy has not always been appropriate. The results of wrong decisions are usually negatively reflected in the company's balance sheet.

COM STRAT lets the user make simulated decisions and get experience in company management in a model example without any real consequences. Decisions of the users after being analysed by the computer model reflect the market situation.

Afterwards the outcomes of the already made decisions are shown as the financial results of the business. This innovative method of teaching is offered by both the curriculum of Rzeszów Business School and that of the College of Computer Sciences and Management.

As the result of a competition organized by the PHARE Partnership Programme, the Association of Entrepreneurship Promotion has been chosen to run a project, whose aim is to draw up and implement a model called "cooperation of SMEs with big EU enterprises as part of their internationalzation". The programme concerns two regions of Poland: the north-western one, which has economic contacts with Germany, Denmark and the Scandinavian countries, and the south-east part of Poland which has economic relations with Ukraine, Slovakia, Russia, and Belarus. The partners in the project will be the Western Pomeranian School of Business in Scenic and the Danish Technological Institute.

The core of the project is the preparation of regional business and business networks to perform business activities in the European Community to support economic exchange between the East and the West.

The Business College of the Association of Entrepreneurship Promotion set up four new Business Colleges, besides the already existing ones in Jarosław and Dębica, in Leżajsk, Mielec, Przemyśl and Sanok. The Business College also provides education in administration.

The Association of Entrepreneurship Promotion has also started cooperating with the Western Pomeranian School of Business to organize a series of training programmes in Poland entitled "Managerial Studies" for middle-level executives. The Fachhochschule Dortmund in Germany has drawn up the course and prepared the didactic materials.

The Association of Entrepreneurship Promotion and Bell Leasing Ltd. in Warsaw have drawn up the principles of their cooperation. On the basis of an agreement between these two institutions, the Rzeszów Network of Business Support Centres has become the representative of Bell Leasing in south-eastern Poland. Using the experience of highly qualified advisory staff as well as a wide variety of technical equipment, Rzeszów Network of Business Support Centres will promote among its customers the ideas and advantages of leasing as a convenient form of financing an investment and it will sign leasing contracts on behalf of Bell Leasing. A new network of constantly cooperating suppliers of investment goods will be created. Both partners, i.e. the Association of Entrepreneurship Promotion and Bell Leasing are interested in long-term cooperation and their experience so far looks promising.

On the grounds of the agreement between the Association of Entrepreneurship Promotion and Credit - Deposit Bank Inc. in Lublin, the Rzeszów Business School has conducted training for bank employees, entitled "The quality (culture) of bank service".

Services provided by the SME – Business Support Centre and the Euro Info Centre

As an example we would like to show how the BSC and EIC operate in Podkarpackie province and their regular methods of work.

The network of Business Support Centres was created as a part of the Project for Supporting Small and Medium-Sized Enterprises, and the Programme of Private Sector Development. Both were implemented with the use of financial support granted by the European Community (PHARE Programme). The Association of Entrepreneurship Promotion became a host structure for this network.

The BSC offers a wide range of services in the following areas:
- preparation of internal and external business plans for companies
- financial analysis of investment ventures
- programmes for improving and restructuring business enterprises
- international trade
- marketing
- taxation and legal advice
- advisory services for municipalities
  - preparation of development strategy
  - programmes for promoting municipalities and regions
  - training in the area of promotion.

The Euro Info Centre hosted by the Association of Entrepreneurship Promotion was created as an Euro Info Correspondence Centre Regional Representative office in 1995. In 1998 the European Commission decided to create 12 independent Euro Info Centres in Poland. In 1999 the EIC was established by the Association of Entrepreneurship Promotion. The main objective of the EIC is to prepare Polish small and medium-sized companies for joining the European Union and for operating on the Single European market. The EIC has more than 250 active clients.

Our EIC offers a wide range of services including:

- market information for EU countries
- assistance to enterprises in contacting partners through the EIC network operating in all EU countries
- providing SMEs with detailed information concerning EU legislation and quality standards
- information about EU programmes and projects for SMEs
- organization and invitations for international events like Europartenariat, Interprise, IBEX.

Romania

After 1990 the activity of the Government has given priority to the privatization and restructuring of large state enterprises. SME supporting programmes were mainly initiated by international donors:
- ➢ non-reimbursable financial allocations for investments (PHARE Programme)
- ➢ access to premises through business incubators
- ➢ consultancy services.

The Government, together with the banks, has set up two guarantee funds: one for private entrepreneurs, the other one for farmers. The legal framework was improved in July 1999 when a new law for the SME sector was passed by the Parliament as Law no.133/1999. The Law regulates the framework concerning:
- ➢ SME definition
- ➢ organization of SME policy
- ➢ main measures to support the SME sector
- ➢ improvement of SME knowledge base
- ➢ support measures, programming and funding for SMEs.

The measures provided by the Law for supporting the SME sector are focused on improving the business environment, and improving SME access to business support services and to credit, as well as to public procurement and the business industrial infrastructure. They foresaw some tax reductions in cases where profits we would be reinvested by the SMEs.

At present, the Law is only partially in force because some important provisions have not been applied yet, having been temporarily suspended.

Recognizing the importance of the SME sector as one of the main instruments for promoting accession to the European Union, the Government developed "The National Strategy on SME Sector Development". This document was submitted to the EC.

The general objectives of the government strategy aim to maximize the contribution of the SME sector to:
- ➢ the creation of new jobs
- ➢ sustainable economic growth
- ➢ improving the competitiveness of the economy
- ➢ the development of a middle class.

According to the Law, the formulation, implementation and coordination of SME policy was assigned to the National Agency for Small and Medium Enterprises - NASME established in December 1998. In May 2000 NASME was included as a department within the National Agency for Regional Development.

The development of the SME sector in Romania is supported by a wide range of institutions and organizations such as:
- ➢ chambers of commerce and industry
- ➢ business incubator centres
- ➢ international organizations; World Bank, United Nations Development Programme, United Nations, USAID
- ➢ business information centres : EuroInfo Centres, Trade and Technological Promotion Information System (TIPS), Trade Point, Trade Information Network of Chambers of Commerce of Group 77 countries
- ➢ financial institutions and intermediates (guarantee funds, banks etc.);

- business advisory and counselling centres
- business associations and organizations operating as NGOs: Romanian National Committee for Private Small and Medium-sized Enterprises, Romanian Association of Women Managers etc.
- foundations and development centres for SMEs setup by UNDP, PHARE and United Nations projects;

Role of the Chambers of Commerce and Industry in the promotion and development of SMEs

The chambers of commerce and industry are organized according to a specific law. They are non-Governmental, autonomous, non-profit and self-financing. There are 42 local chambers, one for each county. The Chamber of Commerce and Industry of Romania functions as both the national chamber and the Bucharest chamber. Membership is voluntary.

According to the law the mission of the chambers is to:
- support the development of its members' activities;
- represent the interests of the business community before the Government and Parliament.

New tasks and competencies have been assigned to the chambers by the SME Law. The most important being:

- elaboration, in cooperation with the central and local public administration, of the policy for simplifying the bureaucratic formalities concerning SME establishment and development;
- keeping records of the available assets belonging to large State companies;
- supporting the SME business consultancy and information centres network;
- involvement in the entrepreneurs management training programmes;
- advising on the elaboration of programmes dedicated to SMEs.

Business advisory, counselling and information services provided by the Chambers

The Chambers' services have been defined taking into consideration the life cycle of the enterprise, containing four main stages:

- establishment
  - preparatory activities for setting-up and registration required by law;
- development-maturity
  - including activities focused on the development of enterprises related to business induction, business preparation and launching, partnership development, and exports
- decline and growth crises
  - analysis
  - restructuring
  - innovation and upgrading of technologies
- activity cessation and death
  - dissolution, liquidation and removal from the Trade Register.

Services rendered

Services are especially focused on the initial business advisory and counselling services related to the establishment and development-maturity of the enterprise, as well as to activity cessation and company death.

Professional consultancy is generally provided by specialized companies excepting unfair competition and commercial arbitration that, by law, are in the chambers' competence.

The services offered consist of:
- assistance in setting up the trading companies and amending the by-laws
- consulting on advice, licences, authorization for some activities and obtaining advice
- information on available rental space and assets
- information on existing opportunities and projects

- primary consulting on business financing possibilities
- advice on fiscal matters: taxes, duties and related fiscal charges and customs matters
- advice in employment matters and relations with chambers of labour
- organization of fairs and exhibitions
- organization of economic missions, business meetings, partnerships in Romania and overseas
- information concerning participation in public tenders
- guidance in relation to foreign markets
- issues related to EU integration
- identifying partners in the EU
- financial assistance from EU institutions
- participation in EU programmes and European tenders
- protection for intellectual and industrial property rights, prevention and avoidance of counterfeits
- organization of courses, seminars, conferences
- use of ATA carnet during the temporary transport of goods.

Business information services

The Chamber of Commerce and Industry of Romania is the initiator, main designer and manager of:
- the legal register of companies containing data on 800.000 entities, available on the Internet
- business information including companies profiles, opportunities, trade fairs and exhibitions
- ABC Net (Business Information Network of Balkan Chambers)
- Internet databases
- CD-ROM annual version - PRO BUSINESS ROMANIA.

Electronic commerce and the Chambers of Commerce and Industry

This objective was approached from two main directions:

- to facilitate increased competitiveness and participation in global trade for SMEs by exploiting the opportunities offered by the development of the Global Information Society;
- to adapt the internal organization of the chambers and human resources to the new system for delivering services using web call centres, e-business solutions and WAP technologies based on the large use of the Internet and e-mobile.
- The role of the chambers and the activities carried out in the e-commerce are:
  - to make entrepreneurs aware of using the Internet and e-commerce tools;
  - to facilitate e-commerce projects by using global networks or designing their own projects;
  - to develop new business information and counselling services based on new ITC tools.
- The main services they have developed up to now in the field of e-commerce:
  - the provision of digital signature and digital certificate, the Chambers being the national registration authority within the work of the G77 on the e-trade model through strategic alliances with key international companies and organizations (TIN CCI/G77);
  - the setting up of the central Trade Register as the portal for e-commerce.

Call Centre

This service was designed for the efficient management and support of client relationships. It offers professional services 24 hours a day and 7 days a week to the persons interested in information on the Chamber's products, services, and activities. The client can also lodge complaints about the quality of some services or products or make recommendations.

The Call Centre is not only an information point but also a method for analysing the clients' opinion on services. It is a "one-stop-shop" for assisting beginners in starting up their businesses.

A one-stop-shop is the functional structure on the principle of offering at one place packages of services required by Romanian or foreign investors who wish to set up and develop businesses in Romania.

It is a "friendly interface" between investors and administrative barriers in the business environment having as its objective diminishing the negative effects resulting from bureaucracy, lack of information and legislative incoherence.

It was designed to be the first gateway opened for the entrepreneur towards the business environment.

Its objectives include:
➤ reducing the period of adjustment for an investor to the features of the business environment (legislation, business information, opportunities);
➤ reducing costs;
➤ reducing the time spent to initiate and develop the business;
➤ eliminating contacts with administrative institutions;
➤ focusing the investor more on business than on the bureaucratic procedures.

The legal framework for the one-stop-shop approach is defined in:
➤ Government Decision no 941/ 1995 was the first legal provision for establishing one-stop-shop activities;
➤ Ordinance no 32/1997 for modification of the Law no 31/1990 concerning companies provides for the simplification of formalities for establishing a company and it introduces the obligation of trade registry offices to send "ex-officio" the required paper for publication in the Official Gazette;
➤ Law no 133/1999 concerning the setting-up and the development of SMEs contains two provisions, entitling the chamber of commerce and industry to:

- implement the unique procedure for SMEs registration at the trade registry office;
- introduce a simplified procedure for getting the licences and authorization for certain activities through the BASCD bureau for assisting with the establishment and development of enterprises.

Russian Federation

According to Goskomstat, there were 897,000 small and medium businesses in the Russian Federation, employing more than 7 million workers at the beginning of 1999. The amount of GDP produced by small businesses in Russia is much smaller than in the developed market economies of the West. Nevertheless, small-scale entrepreneurship is particularly strong in Russia's two capitals, Moscow and St Petersburg as well as Nizhnii Novgorod, cities like Perm and Novosibirsk, where there is a large pool of skilled workers, and Saratov, where regional authorities support it. It is possible to find examples of thriving small businesses in a wide variety of regions.

The common thread that runs through success stories is the ability of the firm to make or resell relatively high-quality products at low prices. Producing something that is almost as good as an expensive import, but at a fraction of the cost, is particularly effective, even if it is slightly more expensive than cheaper but shoddy domestic products. Many successful businesses started out importing foreign goods and then learned how to make something similar in Russia. The best small businesses often use foreign equipment to work with Russian materials.

Both new and seasoned entrepreneurs face a number of problems on whose solution depend not only the future of their business, but also the well-being of their families.

The main obstacles to success for small businesses are taxes and poor relations with the regional and local authorities. The adoption of the federal law on imputed incomes on 31 July 1998 has proven to be a disaster. The idea was to make it easier to collect taxes from small businesses, which often hide their sales and therefore pay less to the State budget than they should by law. However, the new law gives regional officials wide discretion in how to implement the tax and many regions have raised the amount of money small businesses must pay, driving lots of them out of business and increasing unemployment.

Bureaucratic regulation also creates enormous problems for the business community. Many Moscow store owners complain that they suffer frequent inspections by officials seeking payments.

The Nizhny Novgorod newspaper Birzha recently published the results of a poll asking local entrepreneurs about administrative barriers in business. Administrative barriers are defined as an existing set of registration, licensing, certification, standardization requirements and the rest of the various supervising and controlling organs. Which under the slogan of "care and protection of citizens' rights, health and life" require small businesses to expend unbearable amounts of time, effort and resources.

Overall, the entrepreneurs believe that the current political elite in Russia lives in a different world and is not able to adopt normal laws. There is some hope that the situation will improve in several years.

The four main problems that the entrepreneurs identified are taxes, the "State racket," the lack of qualified managers, weak financial support, and the lack of information. The problem with taxes is that there are too many of them. Discussing the amount of taxes only is like determining the size of an iceberg by its above-water part. The problems are hidden in the whole State tax system.

Besides, due to its specifics, a small enterprise is unable to create specialized departments, such as Finance, Legal, Consulting, Marketing, Informational, and Educational, as most large companies usually can.

Executive authorities currently act irrespective of the existing reality. Uncontrolled activities of financial pyramids and the irresponsible servicing of the government's private debts undermine trust in Government structures. Entrepreneurs have formed a generally negative opinion towards any, even to those seemingly attractive, decisions of the authorities. For instance, the Presidential Decree "On elimination of administrative barriers" correctly reflects the scope of the problem; however, newly adopted regulations (the law "On grain and the products of its processing" and the draft law "Quality and security of food products"), contradict the aforementioned Decree. They just strengthen administrative barriers, create new obstacles for small business development and cause business to react negatively. This is why in countries where small business is widely common, which includes practically all of the civilized world, public organizations take charge of creating a small business infrastructure, which includes a whole system of specialized organizations whose goal is to promote the interests of SMEs, to satisfy the needs of small enterprises and to create favourable conditions and take into consideration the specific requirements of SMEs.

The State at the federal level is unwilling to and, therefore, is not working on the creation and support of both the required infrastructure and the area of small entrepreneurship. International and donor organizations are basically responsible for the initiation of small entrepreneurship infrastructure creation in Russian. However, this has resulted in parallel structures in different regions due to a lack of coordination as regards the implementation of different rules. Most of the existing infrastructure organizations claim to be multifunctional. Just looking at a typical flyer of a similar company is enough to see that the company deals in consulting, business planning, marketing, information support, education and establishing business contacts with Western partners, investment planning and leasing. Taking into consideration the fact that all these companies usually do not have more than 5-6 people on the payroll, it becomes evident that all these claims make no sense whatsoever. At the same time these companies try to compete with each other instead of occupying their own niche on the service market and cooperating.

However, the whole thing is perhaps not so bad as it would seem at first sight. There are positive examples of small entrepreneurship support and development at the federal and regional levels.

The federal laws connected with the problems of administrative barriers to licensing, and customers' cooperative societies were passed in the summer of 2001. This can be treated as a sign of growing interest by the authorities and the Government in the practical work in an economy in transition.

The 1990s saw the start-up of a multitude of business associations, whose key goal was to secure that interests of various businesses would be taken into account in the State decision-making process. Issues of small business support and development were incorporated in the programmes of a majority of political parties and movements represented in the State Duma. Still, here is a key policy challenge. Advocacy which is a key for the future development of the business climate, is not yet properly functioning in Russia. Specifically, though the Chamber of Commerce is usually involved in lobbying business interests, its role is not so great here as, for example, in a number of European countries.

The last decade witnessed the emergence of a few major business support institutions, including the Russian Agency for SME Support, the Russian Association of SME Development, and the Morozov Project. These institutions sprang up owing to active support on the part of the Russian Government and international programmes; at present they are key players in the market for business services, and they actively participate in fashioning a national policy in this area.

A multitude of foreign and international institutions – the Russia Small Business Fund, the European Bank for Reconstruction and Development, the US Agency for International Development, the Eurasia Foundation, the TACIS Programme and others – provide a considerable amount of resources for the development of business in Russia.

The Russian Agency for Small and Medium Business Support (RA) is currently a major consulting company for SMEs in the Russian Federation. It was set up in late 1992 on the initiative of the Government, with the support of the Know How Fund of the United Kingdom. Its primary objective was to provide practical assistance in establishing and developing small and medium businesses, and the promotion of entrepreneurship.

At present this Agency performs a wide range of consulting services for both new and advanced entrepreneurs that cover legal information, business-planning, taxes and finance, credit facilities, optimization of tax payments, marketing research, registration services, training, promotion of commercial offers through SIORA_net, information services, as well as searches for partners, for specific information on products and services, and information on donor organizations.

To promote and lobby the common interests of Russian small and medium business the SMEDAs Association «Razvitie» was set up in 1997. It now embraces about 40 regional agencies and is expanding its activities both vertically and horizontally in accordance with its Board's plans.

To deliver wider assistance to SMEs, the Agency has signed a number of agreements with the Federal Fund for Small Business Support, the Federal Employment Service, the Fund for the Support of Small Business Innovation, the Academy of Management and Markets (Morozov Project).

One of the functions of the Agency is to assist public structures in finding adequate ways to develop small business in Russia. The Agency works in close cooperation with the Ministry of Anti-monopoly policy and Entrepreneurship support, the Federal Fund for Small Business Support, the Chamber of Commerce and Industry of the Russian Federation and various SME associations. Particularly, the Agency provides expertise on small business legislation which is discussed in the State Duma Committees and other State institutions.

The Business Communication Centre (BCC) of the Russian Agency for SME support was set up within the framework of the project TACIS SMERUS9602. The establishment and development of the BCC played an important role in the activities of the RA: the range of services offered by the RA was extended, the quality of the original services provided by the departments of the RA was improved; it assisted in establishing a network of regional agencies for SME support and in promoting their interaction.

Lobbying for the interests of small business development through federal and regional authorities has always been a major task of the Russian agency and then of the "Razvitie" Association since the very beginning of the reforms Inadequate and unstable support from the Government and other public structures to small business in recent years has given birth to the idea of the Second Russian SME Congress as a very useful lobbying vehicle. A Steering Committee comprising leaders of the Russian Agency, the RF Chamber of Commerce/Industry, the Association of SME development and regional SME actors undertook the preparation of the Congress. Its primary objective was to revise State policy for small entrepreneurship development and make it a priority for Russian economic reform. The

Congress adopted a resolution with concrete proposals on SME support and development in Russia. It was submitted to the Government, the State Duma, the Council of Federation and other State bodies.

A special sitting of the Government was then dedicated to SME problems. A decision was adopted about the steps to support small business. The decision overall approves the idea and the draft of the federal programme for SME State (public) support for 2000-2001. It instructs relevant governmental bodies to expand the range of institutional support to protect effective SME development, to define models of extrabudgetary SME financing, to correlate domestic and foreign programmes for SME support, etc. The updated federal support programme is to be submitted to the State Duma for final approval.

Important tasks in the area of institutional support include updating the federal law of May 1995 "On State support of SMEs in the Russian Federation" and the elaboration of regulations on tax reduction for SME entities, access to affordable non-banking finance, franchising, venture financing, elimination of administrative barriers and others.

Regardless, recent Governmental decisions adopted as follow-up to the SME Congress present a real break through in the prevailing federal authorities' attitudes towards SME development.

In general, the idea of systematic work with small businesses is becoming quite popular in Russia, confirmed by attempts to localize all entire small business support activities in Moscow, Nizhny Novgorod, Ekaterinburg, Vladimir and other regions through SMEDAs or other structures. If the federal authorities support these efforts at least legally and administratively, and international and donor organizations provide adequate technical assistance, small business is likely to become a significant asset for the Russian economy.

The introduction of the Internet into the Russian market was a real breakthrough. Coupled with the efforts made at the first stage by international and donor organizations such as TACIS, the Soros Foundation, Eurasia Fund, USAID, UNIDO and others, it opened up new vistas for the development of relevant technologies and for information exchange. Dozens and later hundreds of Russian firms dealing with pertinent issues sprang up and started to adopt best practices in the field as well as create purely Russian products geared to local conditions.

The Federal Programme "Electronic Russia" was approved in summer 2001. In addition, during the past few years, Russia has already developed at least 4 national Internet networks for servicing the interests of businessmen in terms of commercial information, which are worth mentioning here. They are as follows:

➢ Russian BCNet, the network based on regional chambers of commerce and industry (CCI) and initiated by RF. It contains information of a commercial, analytical and operational nature but the bottleneck in this system is that it consists of fragmentary databases, very rarely updated and unpardonably expensive. Besides, the operation of different CCIs in the regions varies greatly, which is reflected in the information resources that they are able to provide.

➢ The Morozov Project, which was started by USAID and some other donor organizations in cooperation with a number of Russian higher education institutions as an attempt to organize knowledge transfer and experience sharing throughout Russia on the basis of regional centres. At a later stage it introduced into the Internet some of its resources most of which are of an educational and consultative nature. The third phase, 2001 – 2004, has been launched.

➢ SMEDA Network, which is supported by TACIS through different projects and typically oriented towards providing basic or even sophisticated services and consultancy, in general, to SMEs. SIORA Net, which unites some of the agencies in the network, seems to be a typical example of a horizontal web-site according to the tasks it states as crucial: to provide multiple consultancy, distant inclusive, to improve managerial skills of SMEs, to integrate them into the international community, to give them access to investment, to offer SMEs marketing services of a broad range, to provide State bodies and institutions with analytical and other information relevant to SME development, to help formulate State policy in the SME field to both the federal and the regional Governments, etc. Such a broad spectrum of tasks prevents agencies, especially in the regions, from covering thoroughly any of the goals set, since their staff does not exceed 3-5 people.

➢ Last but not the least, is the Interregional Marketing Centres Network (the IMC Network), the project initiated by the Moscow Government, but which two years later was evaluated as an all-Russian one both within Russia and abroad. This Network of information and marketing companies helps business persons and enterprises from different locations to establish direct contacts, to determine the actual needs of regions and territories for goods and services, to promote the diversification of local markets and, to this end, to manage and keep up-to-date distributed databases on producers, their opportunities and their products.

Within the infrastructure for SME support in Russia, the Russian SME Resource Centre (RCSME), a non-commercial foundation initially established under the Tacis program, performs research on SME development and provides policy advisory services and information support to the small and medium-sized business community.

Within the framework of the Tacis programme the RCSME developed a Web-site (www.rcsme.ru) that is a helpful information and analytical resource for the business support community in all Russia's regions. In order to promote business cooperation of Russian and foreign SMEs at the international level a Russian web-site (http://baltic.rcsme.ru) of the Baltic SME portal for trade and investment (in English) was developed by the RCSME.

System Projects of IMC Network

Each Interregional Marketing Centre (IMC) participates in information exchange with the other centres involved, and observes corporate standards of information and marketing activities as they have been established over the entire Network. Thus, IMCs act within a unified information space and practice a shared methodology for marketing surveys. Each local IMC develops partnership relations with other information and marketing companies, as well as the information and statistics departments of local administrations. Such collaboration helps collect and process the most up-to-date information on the business environment and the latest commercial opportunities on the local market.

Distributed Interregional Database

IMC "Moscow" administers the central server of the IMC information network where statistical, economic and commercial information from the Network's regional centres is accumulated. Similar information units are created in regions under the administration of local IMCs. Thus, information is being collected in unified formats and it constitutes a single distributed database, the latter being offered to business persons in search of partners or markets in other regions. Currently this information bank contains data on enterprises interested in interregional cooperation, as well as on their commercial opportunities. The software used therein provides search engines, classifiers and analytical tools.

Databases on investment projects and wholesale prices in Russian regions have also been created.

Electronic Catalogue of Regional Products

The business community in this country has always felt a shortage of data on locally produced goods. The necessity of such information became even more evident after the financial crisis of 1998, when decreased imports failed to meet the internal demand for ready-made goods. The public database project on regional production is intended to compensate for the lack of information of this kind. The "Catalogue of Goods and Services" contains detailed descriptions of the properties and characteristics of the represented consumer goods, some graphic representations of every item and links to delivery conditions and the address information provided by the manufacturer. The information for the catalogue is collected by the local centres, thus promoting the production of the enterprises of the particular region onto the All-Russia market. The Catalogue is published in the section "Databases" on the web site www.marketcentre.ru .

Virtual Offices for Small and Medium-Sized Businesses

IMC Network has started to develop a new version of its official web site that is now based on a 'sale of services' model rather than a 'sale of information' model. In particular, the virtual space of the site will be turned into a kind of 'business centre' where any user can rent a virtual office (VO). A VO differs from traditional web representation, as it has a special working area available, to which only employees of the "tenant" organization have access. Here official correspondence and discussion forums, tools for teamwork on projects and internal documents may be located. The "Virtual Secretary" enters and processes messages, and maintains mailing lists, with maximum efficiency using the advantages of membership in the community of VO owners. For the external user, the VO looks like an interactive, dynamically formed web site. VOs are structured according to a geographical attribute: offices of the Interregional Marketing Centres "rent out" a part of their space to regional businessmen. According to some estimates, the number of potential users of such a portal should increase from 14,790 persons in 2000 up to 87,000 persons in 2002.

The purpose of the project is to make available the new opportunities for establishing economic ties inside and outside Russia to manufacturers selling and purchasing equipment. To create such opportunities we use the IMC Network, which is present in the majority of the large cities in Russia for rendering information and advertising services. We also use Internet-technologies for the centralised collecting and processing of client orders for managing advertising campaigns, and for offering marketing services on-line as well. The initiative consists in accompanying commercial one-line publications in the popular "Optovik" magazine with a full advertising package situated within the electronic services of the IMC information network, so that readers know where to look for details on items that attracted them most.

Complex Programme of Information Support for Businesspersons and Manufacturers of Business Equipment

This project is aimed at assisting businesspersons in and outside Russia in receiving information about equipment and industrial components they are interested in and to assist manufacturers and suppliers of the equipment to find buyers. An information package on every item in the list of the proposed equipment, including address information, is created by our customer with the help of IMC experts and may contain textual, graphic, photo and video materials. Then, if necessary, it is duplicated and sent to one or more remote IMCs chosen by the customer. Public access to the formed database is open through regional information units and through the central server of the corporate network. Alternatively, an entrepreneur in need of

equipment may receive information on the desired machinery upon request, having visited a local IMC and having taken advantage of a library of "hard copies" or by means of video films. Delivery of information is guaranteed and free of charge. The businesspersons searching for particular equipment are provided with a full information package prepared by the customer. An end consumer pays charges only for copying materials.

Monitoring of Wholesale Prices in the Russian Regions

The project has been developed for the purpose of granting easy access to information on wholesale prices in various regions of Russia to a broad business audience. The information collected through this project is updated every two weeks. It is free and obtained directly through the participation of employees of the regional centres. The software developed for the monitoring database allows you not only to make and print reports on a certain date, but also to analyse data on chosen groups of goods in dynamics and in a regional basis. These data really help businesspeople to analyse the price situation in various regions. The project has been under way since April 1999.

Interregional Business Advertising and Direct Marketing Service based on the IMC Network

This project is designed to create essentially new opportunities for marketing communications and promoting products in Russia's regions by means of direct marketing via traditional advertising media. The project included:
  ➢ creating a database of regional mass media;
  ➢ using the information network of the IMCs for supplying complex advertising and marketing services;
  ➢ use of regional advertising media and handbooks as a basis for customer commercial publications;
  ➢ making use of Internet technologies for the centralized gathering and processing of customer orders.

All the projects described above should help considerably in bridging the gap in information experienced by Russian businesspeople, especially at the interregional level. All of the projects require action within more or less one niche and combine the use of advanced technologies with traditional ones, which is very important as the population in the distant regions of Russia still have difficulties in getting access to the Internet.

All IMCs also promote goods and services in outside markets for regional companies that wish to outsource these kinds of activity. The fact that they operate using the same standards and technologies facilitates the interaction of businesses throughout the territory of Russia. The Network covers the major part of the Russian Federation territory, which makes it attractive to similar foreign systems and opens up prospects for international cooperation in this field.

Slovakia

Information, counselling and training services for SMEs are provided by institutional support network. The network was built up gradually during 1993 - 1996 with the main mission of supporting development of the SME sector in the Slovak Republic. At present network consists of the National Agency for Development of Small and Medium Enterprises, 12 Regional Advisory and Information Centres and 5 Business and Innovation Centres.

National Agency for Development of Small and Medium Enterprises

The National Agency for Development of Small and Medium Enterprises (NADSME) was founded as a joint initiative of the PHARE programme of the European Union and the Government of Slovakia in 1993. It coordinates the activities supporting small and medium enterprises and facilitates the coordination of

support provided to the SME sector in Slovakia by PHARE.

The main aim of the Agency is to initiate and coordinate the development and growth of existing and newly formed small and medium enterprises.

Activities of the Agency are divided into three main areas:

a) SME policy and development

The agency carries out activities to support the development of new Government policies and strategies. It identifies barriers and problems to SME development, prepares and submits drafts proposals with possible solutions to the relevant bodies. It also monitors the entrepreneurial environment and the development of the SME sector.

b) Information and counselling

The main objective of the information and counselling programme is to provide SMEs with a complete service through the network of Regional Advisory and Information centres (RAICs), Business and Innovation Centres, as well as through the services of "Sub-contracting Exchange of Slovakia" and Euro-Info Centre.

c) Financial Support Programmes

The financial support programmes facilitate SMEs access to capital by providing them with soft loans and credits. At present the Agency runs credit programmes, microloan schemes and a seed capital fund.

Since 1993 NADSME has started several specialized subsidiary operations such as Subcontracting Exchange of Slovakia, Euro-Info Centre, Trade Centre and others.

In order to provide professional information and advisory services to small and medium-sized entrepreneurs the Agency has created an institutional network. It includes Regional Advisory and Information Centres (RAIC) and

Business and Innovation Centres (BIC) and their branch offices throughout Slovakia.

The RAICs and BICs were established by the Government of the Slovak Republic and the European Union within the framework of the PHARE Small and Medium Enterprises Programme for the Czech and Slovak Federal Republic signed in October 1991.

The centres were created in select areas which complied with the following criteria:
> a priority region in which an industrial restructuring was going on and therefore a lot of jobs were lost
> in large centres offering a potential for the development of modern innovative enterprises

Three pilot RAICs and one BIC were set up in 1992. Between 1993 and 1996 the network expanded to 12 RAICs and 5 BICs.

Regional Advisory and Information Centres (RAICs)

RAICs represent local advisory entrepreneurial agencies. Their mission is to assist in the creation of new, and the development of existing SMEs and thus contribute to the development of the respective regions. The RAICs were established as associations of legal entities on the basis of a partnership between the public and the private sectors.

Their main objective is to provide a complete package of support services in all areas related to business. Current services offered by the RAICs are:
> Appraisal of entrepreneurial business plans with a view to increasing the possibility for success and reducing the element of risk
> Development of business plans for the support of SMEs for funding from domestic banks and foreign assistance funds
> Advisory and information services necessary for the establishment and successful development of enterprises in the

fields of: management, marketing, financial management, accounting and legislation
> Looking for suitable foreign partners
> Organizing seminars and training for entrepreneurs
> Organizing the complex training-advisory programme "Establishing your own enterprise" for the unemployed, in cooperation with employment agencies

The advisory services, training courses and seminars organized in cooperation with many other institutions and organizations are targeted at the development of individual regions as well as their integration into projects and activities at the international level.

Business and Innovation Centres (BICs)

In 1991 EU submitted a proposal within the PHARE project to establish 3 pilot centres in what was then Czechoslovakia. Prague, Brno and Bratislava were chosen as localities with companies having a big potential for innovation. The objective of the pilot projects was to prove whether BIC activities would have a positive impact on transforming economies.

Based on the advice of the European Business and Innovation Centre Network (EBN) it was recommended to establish a limited liability company (s.r.o.) in Bratislava on a private basis as a spin-off of the research institute. BIC in Slovakia was the first instrument for supporting small and medium-sized enterprises. The conditions for traditional founders of BICs (in the EU these are cities, regions, chambers of commerce and entrepreneurs) did not exist and therefore a variant of a private organization was agreed with possible sale of shares and property arrangements in the future. The BICs are non-profit making organizations established according to the commercial code as limited liability companies, in which the profit is not distributed. If any profit is made, it is utilized for company development and the support of entrepreneurs. The status of limited liability company fully enables BIC activities to be developed and secures the possibility to finance them from grants as well as from their own entrepreneurial activities.

The BIC should contribute to the restructuring, recovery and economic development of the regions by means of:
- ➢ the mobilization of regional potential in technical, scientific, financial, logistical and human resources areas,
- ➢ searching for, evaluating, selecting and orienting such entrepreneurs with innovation projects, who are able to found and conduct their own business, with high potential of added value, supporting entrepreneurs with projects oriented towards the creation of a new entrepreneurial body or a new production process in an existing enterprise.

The main task of the BIC is searching for and selecting small and medium-sized enterprises, or new entrepreneurs, whose business plans are innovative (launching a new product, service or technology). They create favourable conditions for those innovative companies by providing them with special long-term care (2-3 years) and serve as "incubators" helping to reduce inevitable start-up costs.

Regional Advisory and Information Centre Prešov (CRAIC Prešov)

A concrete example of services provided to SMEs by the regional centres is illustrated by the case of RAIC Prešov – a member of the NADSME network, established in 1993 as a non-profit association of legal entities.

The task of the RAIC Prešov as an independent, non-profit organization is to provide services and activities that support and create conditions for the development of small and medium-sized enterprises with the purpose of supporting the social-economic development and the democratization of society in the region of Prešov.

Target client groups

The following are the target client groups:
- ➢ Potential small entrepreneurs
- ➢ Existing small enterprises (up to 50 employees)
- ➢ Existing medium enterprises (up to 250 employees)

Services

The following *services* are offered:
- ➢ *Individual consulting*: The Centre provides its clients with consulting services mainly in the area of marketing and financial management. Creating business plans is a much requested service, especially for start-ups. In the case of special requirements, the Centre is able to identify consulting services by external advisers in any area of business activity.
- ➢ *Training services* are aimed first of all at start-up entrepreneurs. There are two regular training products for this target group. The first one " Start up your own firm " is a comprehensive sixty-day course for potential entrepreneurs. The second helps potential entrepreneurs in the course of a ten-day workshop to learn how to create a viable business plan. In addition, the Centre organizes, on an irregular basis, workshops, seminars, and conferences in accordance with the clients´ needs.
- ➢ *Financial services*: apart from the provision of information about different financial sources, the Centre provides its clients with two financial products, namely the Support Loan Programme and the Micro Loan Programme. While the first one is designed for medium-sized enterprises, the Micro loan programme is aimed at start-ups and small businesses.
- ➢ *Information services* are secured by the Euro-Info Centre (EIC), which was established under the auspices of the European Commission. The EIC is a part of RAIC Prešov providing up-to-date information on the business environment and business contacts and organizing

special seminars, workshops and different business events.

Other activities

RAIC Prešov is involved in many other activities reflecting very often the sophisticated needs of clients. Recently the Centre has been focusing on the establishment of a technological incubator centre. It will be a good opportunity for entrepreneurs with innovative ideas to find proper incubator facilities and comprehensive services including a venture capital fund so that they can develop products with high added value.

The Centre is also active in a special international project that is oriented towards the development of the crafts sector in the region.

As the region is suffering from a lack of foreign investment, a new project for a Service Centre for Foreign Investors is being prepared.

Cooperation with other institutions and authorities

On the regional level

The centre cooperates with all relevant regional institutions that participate in the support of small and medium enterprises (State management, municipalities, financial institutions, development agencies, trade chambers, etc.). It is a member of the Economic board of the District of Prešov.

On the national level

The RAIC Prešov is an active member of the Association of the RAICs and BICs of Slovakia, a member of the network for the support of small and medium enterprises in Slovakia coordinated by the National Agency for the Development of Small and Medium Enterprises. It cooperates closely with the Entrepreneurs' Association of Slovakia and with the Craftsmen Association of Slovakia.

On the international level

The RAIC Prešov is a member of the European regional developing agencies EURADA, which has its seat in Brussels. For its loan activities it is a member of the Microfinance Centre for Middle and East Europe, with its seat in Warsaw. On a bilateral level the Centre has partners in England, Ireland, France, Netherlands, Germany, Poland and Hungary.

Euro Info Centre Prešov

The Euro Info Centre in Prešov officially joined the European network of Euro Info Centres in September 1999. Its host structure is the Regional Advisory and Information Centre Presov, one of the chief institutions in the region supporting the development of small and medium-sized enterprises. The main tasks of an EIC is to inform, assist and help small and medium-sized entrepreneurs at every stage of their development. The EIC Prešov fulfils these tasks and provides services for clients all of eastern Slovakia.

The Centre was established as a result of a call from the European Commission for the creation of information units designed for small and medium enterprises in central and eastern European countries aimed at their integration into the European Union.

The need for strengthening business support activities in the region of eastern Slovakia is determined mainly by its socio-economic situation. While the number of inhabitants living in the region is almost one third of the entire population of Slovakia the socio-economic indicators are not proportional. Equally, unemployment in eastern Slovakia largely exceeds the national average. The Prešov region, together with two others in Slovakia, was thus identified by the Government as regions where the highest financial flows would be directed in the future, whether through Structural Funds tools, i.e. ISPA and SAPARD, regional funds or other financial sources.

Thus it is not surprising that the situation is reflected also by one of the most significant indicators, by the GDP, which represents only 20% of that of the country's production. Equally the region's foreign investment share is much lower here and represents only 12.8 % of the total foreign investment in Slovakia. This unfavourable situation is related to the geographical location of the region in the very east of the country and with the insufficiently developed infrastructure there.

Information Services

On the basis of requests, the EIC provides its clients with information of different content, from the simple cooperation profiles of foreign and Slovak companies to brief marketing reviews as well as information on the current business environment in Slovakia and on European markets.

In order to provide relevant information on SMEs both in the region and throughout Slovakia, especially to foreign companies or institutions, the EIC has been building its own database of companies.

The Centre also uses other information resources such as the commercial register of Slovak companies, the library of official European Commission publications, books and magazines dealing with the issues regarding the European integration process.

Dissemination of information

Since the beginning of its services the EIC in Prešov has been in regular contact with the local newspapers where it regularly publishes business offers from foreign companies, calls for companies to join international projects and information on the latest programmes and initiatives concerning SMEs. In cooperation with the local broadcasting station, the EIC Prešov informs the public about its activities, predominantly about planned regional, national and international events, competitions etc.

The EIC has established its own web site. Apart from the presentation of offered services, information on major events, cooperation offers and others, it enables access to essential information sources of the European Commission. The regular updating of the web site reflects the needs and requirements of entrepreneurs from the

whole area of eastern Slovakia. A special information service designed for companies with Internet connection enables the regular dissemination of up-to-date information to that group of clients.

Organization of workshops and seminars

As part of its assistance to Slovak companies to find their place in European markets and to keep them informed about business matters in Europe the EIC organizes seminars and workshops.

In that manner a series of special seminars dealing with e-commerce applications has been arranged in several towns of the region. Likewise seminars focusing on public procurement and private property were organized for a target group of small and medium-sized enterprises.

Promotion of international cooperation

An equally important activity of the Centre is its assistance in establishing business, production, technological and financial cooperation between Slovak and foreign companies. To accomplish this task the Centre is in permanent contact with the other EICs in the network through the intranet electronic system VANS which enables efficient mutual communication.

EIC is also a national correspondent of the Partner Search Database, an official database with headquarters in Brussels, enabling companies to publicize their cooperation profiles or cooperation requests worldwide.

Participation in international fairs

Within the INTERPRISE programme of the EC the main goal of which is to create opportunities for establishing cooperation contacts between small and medium-sized enterprises from different European countries the EIC Presov acted as a National Counsellor in arranging the participation of Slovak companies in the cooperation fair, EUROPARTNER NRW 2000, the venue of which was the German town of Dortmund. During the two days of this cooperation exchange market, representatives from 14 companies, mainly from the region could carry out direct negotiations with foreign partners from nine European regions.

The same role was played by the Centre in the case of the Economic Forum on Food and Related Sectors held in Bialystok, Poland, in October 2000 and during the cooperation meetings of European companies representing furniture and wood processing industry in Gdansk in April 2001.

<u>Participation in projects</u>

The EIC Prešov, together with a Danish EIC, took part in an international project dedicated to the specification of the legislative conditions for the establishment of enterprises and performance of crafts in their respective countries.

Through participation in a project focused on the "Enhancement of cooperation on the local level", close cooperation with regional and local business support institutions has been initiated. It is based on the use of a common information system located on the information server of the town.

Partnership on a local, regional and national level

The main partners of the Centre are the network of Regional Advisory and Information Centres and Business Innovation Centres mainly within the region, regional branches of Chambers of Commerce and Industry, national institutions such as the Foreign Trade Support Fund, Slovak Investment and Trade Development Agency as well as the Delegation of the European Commission in Slovakia and other local and regional authorities.

Slovenia

The most important activities to support entrepreneurship development in Slovenia are as follows:

➢ Providing quality services in the field of consulting, training and information through the Small Business Support Network (5 Regional Business Centres and 29 Local Business Centres), establishing the entire network, activating local development partnerships and employment initiatives.

➢ Providing financial incentives (credits, guarantee schemes, financial support to start-ups, non-repayable financing of various target groups).

➢ Developing and implementing support programmes for various target groups (developing entrepreneurship and creativeness among young people, encouraging recognition of women with careers, introduction of home and distance work, entrepreneurship in rural areas).

➢ Designing the "anti-bureaucratic programme" for the elimination of bureaucratic obstacles to entrepreneurship.

➢ Promotional support (presentations at fairs and exhibitions in Slovenia and abroad), training for innovators within the scope of the Slovenian Business Innovation Network and organization of an integrated system of support to innovators.

➢ Encouraging the development of incubators and other forms of entrepreneurial infrastructure (business zones).

➢ Acquainting entrepreneurs with the conditions of business operations in the European Union and EU support programmes for small and medium-sized enterprises, information about business opportunities within the EIC Network.

➢ Drawing up and implementing the programme of entrepreneurship support on the territory of the ex -Yugoslavia within the framework of the Stability Pact.

Providers of the above-mentioned activities are Small Business Development Centre (SBDC) with the Small Business Support Network, the Small Business Development Fund (part of incentives funded jointly by the Ministry of Small Business and Tourism and other partners: the

Employment Service of Slovenia, the Ministry of Labour, Family and Social Affairs, the Ministry of Economic Activities, the Ministry of Science and Technology, the Ministry of Agriculture, Forestry and Food, etc.). One of the most significant projects aimed at supporting entrepreneurship is also the project of co-financing of consulting to entrepreneurs on a voucher basis.

Subsidized Consulting System on Voucher Basis

In Slovenia various forms of support to SMEs were anticipated already by the Small Business Act (1991). Initiatives to organize a "voucher" model of subsidized consulting and training already existed in the 1990s. This concept has been to a large extent implemented at the Employment Service of Slovenia in its employment programme which combines consulting, training and financial support for setting up an enterprise. However, these services are anticipated only for a target group among the unemployed.

Owing to a decrease in the number of newly set up business units, encouraging the establishment of the new ones remains one of the key objectives of development policy. Consequently, in 1999 the SBDC and the Employment Service of Slovenia launched an invitation to tender for the project aimed at developing an overall system of promotion of new enterprises by providing consulting support in the first years of operation or later on for new projects for the expansion of business activities.

Voucher system concept

By a voucher system of consulting, a central form of support to entrepreneurship is being created in Slovenia and it covers any individuals in Slovenia who would like to start their own business. In addition to consulting support, other services can be combined and coordinated by a consultant who will cooperate with an entrepreneur from the very beginning and is well acquainted with his business idea, enterprise and development needs

The fundamental significance of a voucher system is that it anticipates the involvement of practically all target groups of entrepreneurs:

1. Start-up entrepreneurs, commencing their business and making their business idea a reality:
   - unemployed (already until present involved in similar, even broader system),
   - still employed, thinking to start their own business activity,
   - young people having gained a formal education (at secondary school, College or University) who can set up technology-oriented enterprises.

2. Existing enterprises, comprising mainly the following two groups:
   - enterprises with a large-scale development project (extension of business operations, quality upgrading),
   - enterprises facing business difficulties.

We would like to offer vouchers to entrepreneurs on the whole territory of Slovenia and thus make this instrument accessible to entrepreneurs in all regions.

Forms of consulting support to start-ups are:

1. The consulting interview in which an entrepreneur presents his business idea, possibilities and resources. At this point an entrepreneur is integrated into the consulting support system (obtains the first vouchers).
2. This is followed by an introductory seminar on possible forms of support and enterprise business operations.
3. Entrepreneurs take part in a workshop for market analysis and prepare market evaluation of their business idea.
4. Individuals with a prospective business idea attend a workshop on business plan

preparation (supported by a consultant) and draw up their own business plan in a form and manner appropriate for obtaining an agreement on business financing.

5. Entrepreneurs with a virtual business idea register their company and at registration they are assisted by a consultant.

6. During the first operating year the consultant follows the enterprise intensively, identifies possible problems and directs the entrepreneur to the necessary training or other forms of support.

In this system it is essential that for each further step an entrepreneur is obliged to produce a certain consulting "product" which can be evaluated and proves his business maturity and the adequacy of his business idea. If that is not achieved, an entrepreneur can no longer enjoy further consulting support.

Fig 1 – Consulting as a central activity for small business promotion in a voucher system

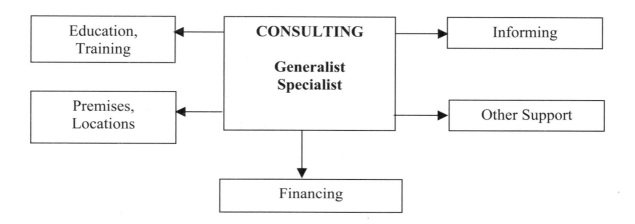

Fig 2 – System Organizations

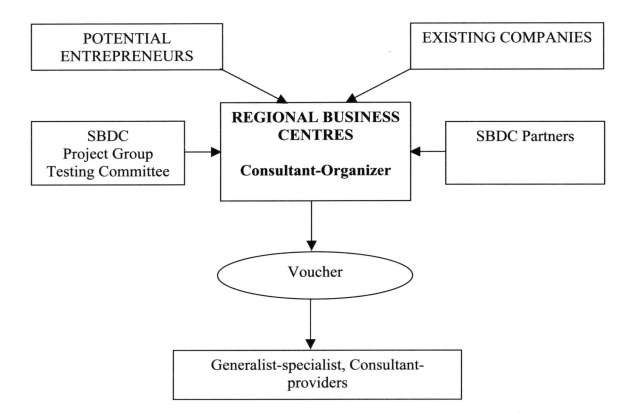

The second group, existing enterprises, will be followed up by consultants until the end of their third operating year. During this period an enterprise is entitled to a certain scope of generalist and specialist consulting. In fact all consulting domains are covered, in particular, needs in the field of finance, marketing, the penetration on complex markets etc. This ensures healthier growth and greater success for enterprises. Subsequently, enterprises are entitled to a certain degree of subsidized consulting at strategic turns or for solving their business difficulties, when creditors are involved. At that point they already participate to a larger extent as regards the co-financing of consulting services support.

System organization

The entire system is based on Regional Business Centres (RBCs) as a convenient system for providing services. An entrepreneur comes to the RBC (on his own initiative or at the suggestion of other partners in the Small Business Support Network) where he is received by a consultant-organizer who studies his business idea and involves him in the system. From the list of generalist and specialist consultants the entrepreneur selects a consultant within the RBC or an external consultant-provider with relevant qualifications and having passed the know-how test. The entrepreneur has the right to make his own choice and also to replace the selected consultant in case he is not satisfied with the consultant's work. Consultants providers in RBCs or other organizations (partners of the Small Business Support Network, consulting firms) provide consulting services within the scope of the standard programme. They are paid for their services upon submission of vouchers signed by entrepreneurs on the basis of an agreed consulting tariff.

Selection of consultants in the system

The voucher system is based on consultants selected at the SBDC level on the basis of a public announcement and know-how test (consulting profiles, criteria and licensing procedure were defined during the development of the SBDC project supported by UNIDO) and have participated in a special training programme for the implementation of the aforementioned system and the execution of consulting tasks.

Follow-up and monitoring of system implementation

To be able to follow-up on this project it is essential to have a quality information system which will be developed in the next year in a Windows application and will be accessible on the Internet. In this way all RBCs would be integrated in a uniform system and the work with entrepreneurs would become a simplified and the system transparent.

Pilot implementation of the system

In the year 2000 the voucher system for consulting was tested in two centres at a regional level, namely in "Dolenjska" and "Koroška". Thus, experience will be accumulated, procedures completed and documentation improved.

Initiation of a voucher system on the whole Slovenian territory

On the basis of experience in the first two regions, a uniform model will be prepared and implemented on the whole territory of Slovenia in the spring of 2002. Promotional activities will also be developed as entrepreneurs will have to be motivated to participate in this new but very interesting project.

The model includes the following:

1. Professional and operationally efficient work of the Project Team under the aegis of SBDC.
2. Selection of qualified consultants.
3. Ensured computer information support for work with entrepreneurs, accounting for services and control of the project operations.
4. Corresponding promotion of the voucher system to target groups of entrepreneurs and enterprises.
5. Established network of Business Centres to organize the consulting system in their territories.
6. Appropriate funds for subsidizing consulting for selected target groups.

The subsidized consulting system is flexible and consequently it's the parameters of its implementation can be determined each year with regard to the organizational capabilities of the network and available funds:

- target groups of entrepreneurs (especially to support integration of particular groups),
- modules included in the voucher system (professionally the most convenient variant is presented),
- scope of subsidized consulting per module (in hours),
- maximum scope of this consulting for consultants-organizers and providers,
- allocation of funds per regions (with an emphasis laid on regions lagging in development) etc.

In addition to operational flexibility it is necessary to assure basic financing, a considerable part of which already in the present system flows in from partners of the Small Business Support Network, and therefore do not represent new funding. At the level of municipalities or regions additional funds for this system can be ensured for target groups of particular importance for them.

Turkey

E-commerce services

KOSGEB, the development organization for SMEs in Turkey, has designed an eCommerce Model with the goal of collecting all SMEs, especially from the manufacturing sector, under one umbrella, building an eMarketplace and enhancing business-to-business relations among SMEs. On the other hand, KOSGEB has signed a convention with DG Enterprise of the EC about eight years ago, to set up the Euro Info Centre as the national contact point in Turkey.

E-Commerce and eBusiness are considered to be important services within the EIC service policy of DG Enterprise. In this respect, the scope and the mission of the KOSGEB eCommerce model has been developed and revized to be compatible with the new service policy of DG Enterprise.

Since eCommerce is a process composed of many activities, the KOSGEB eCommerce Model has been planned to accomplish this process through an information network; namely KOBINET.

KOBINET has been designed in order to provide all the services covered by the eCommerce process. Moreover KOBINET functions as the national subnetwork of the KOSGEB Euro Info Centre. The services envisaged to be provided to enterprises through an eMarketplace are as follows:
  ➢ to provide trade information to SMEs through an information bank,
  ➢ to match supply and demand in an electronic environment,
  ➢ to provide the services to assist in making the first business contacts,
  ➢ to provide a Web page and an e-mail address for each enterprise,
  ➢ to guide and assist the SMEs in developing a detailed web site and establishing business-to-business relations,
  ➢ to establish the organizational and technical infrastructure of an eMarketplace,
  ➢ to present the backoffice services of an eMarketplace to the SMEs.

The basic components of the KOSGEB eCommerce Model can be summarized as follows:
  ➢ business information portal services,
  ➢ e-Mail Services for participating enterprises,

  ➢ web hosting services for enterprises to promote their business,
  ➢ business-to-business and business-to-client services
  ➢ eMarketplace Services for enterprises,
  ➢ The first three components of the model already exist and two more are on the way. B2B services will be developed in 2002.

KOBINET

KOBINET has been formed to develop, encourage, support and spread the use of eCommerce for the purpose of establishing an eMarketplace for enterprises by: advertising them internationally, supporting them in forming and developing business associations with other companies globally, and also by providing access to the information needed for these purposes.

Since it is developed to provide services to SMEs in all business sectors and in all regions, KOBINET is a network formed under the supervision and coordination of KOSGEB with the involvement of civil society organizations and state organizations that provide services to SMEs. Organizations that are providing information include:
  ➢ Public institutions,
  ➢ Chambers of Commerce and Industry,
  ➢ Financial institutions,
  ➢ Business Associations, Foundations, Unions, etc.

As specified above, there exist two types of services available through KOBINET:

Business Information Web Portal Services

The KOBINET business information databank covers information and financial sources, regulations, Customs Union and EU-Turkey relations, in addition to the information requested by SMEs on the economy and the business world. Moreover, the web pages of KOBINET members, business offers/requests from the 80 countries of the BRE Network and similar information are published. BRE Network is one of the SME Support Initiatives of DG

Enterprise, set up in order to develop transnational cooperation.

KOBINET also provides value added information services to enterprises, such as profiles of foreign companies, international tender calls, EU legislation, and CE marking within the context of Euro Info Centre (EIC) services.

Information on Turkish companies in KOBINET is searchable in five languages (English, French, German, Spanish and Italian) as well as Turkish.

The web page services of KOBINET are regularly getting hits from almost 300 centres in the EIC Network.

e-Commerce services

Within the context of eCommerce services, SMEs can fill in the membership application form by connecting to the KOBINET Web Site (www.kobinet.org.tr) and entering their company information (name, address, tel, fax, turnover, employee, products/services, etc.), specifying a user ID and password themselves. This application form is then transmitted to the KOBINET database, and then the authorized personnel of KOSGEB EIC complete the necessary checks and confirm the application.

After validation, a lifelong KOBINET e-mail address and standard web pages in six languages are created automatically for each enterprise. Following the confirmation of their user ID and password, a KOBINET member can start to access all services including web page hosting, web mail, etc. KOBINET members have the possibility of building their web site via the web page hosting service. Through the web mail service, enterprises can reach their e-mails and reply to them from all over the world.

Another important feature of KOBINET is that it offers the possibility to SMEs to update their information and web pages themselves. Once a KOBINET member changes his/her company information in the Turkish web page, this change

is automatically reflected in the web pages of other languages. That's why the KOBINET company database is the most up-to-date of all the SME databases in the country.

KOBINET outreach

Some statistics concerning KOBINET members and usage of KOBINET:
- Presently, there are 10,500 KOBINET members,
- 70% of the members are from industrially developed regions,
- 75% of the members are from the manufacturing sector,
- 5,700 members have Internet a direct access from an ISP, the remaining 4,800 are using dial-up connection in order to connect KOBINET,
- Approximately 6,200 members are using KOBINET actively for mail and databank services,
- KOBINET members are sending and receiving about 150,000 e-mails per month among themselves,
- About 3,000 web pages were updated by enterprises during 2001,
- E-mail traffic is about 250 e-mails/day and five e-mails/member/day,
- The number of visitors to the KOBINET web site, totally and monthly is 180,000 and 8,000, respectively.

The EIC has applied to DG enlargement for financial aid from the EU within the context of the Customs Union Agreement and the MEDA Programme in order to develop the eCommerce services of KOBINET. This proposal has been accepted and the financial agreement has been signed between the EC and Turkish Government. The project probably will start in 2002.

Internet Cafés

To address recent developments within the globalization process KOSGEB EIC has decided to establish "Internet Cafés" in industrial areas hosted by chambers of commerce, industrial zones, and sector representative organizations such as associations or unions. In this respect, the first Internet Café in Mersin Small Industrial Site was created in 1999. Currently the number of Internet Cafés has reached 28.

KOSGEB contributes to the NGO that will host the Internet Café, a total of about $6,000 for the procurement of the hardware and communication equipment. With this the NGO can purchase three 3 PCs, 1 modem, 1 printer, 1 UPS for the Internet Café, alongside the Protocol signed with the host organization. Moreover KOSGEB takes care of the pay roll of the expert to be employed in the Café during the first year. The host organization allocates a place for the Café and meets all the communication fees. SMEs have the following opportunities through the Internet Cafés:

> to access the data bank, eBusiness and eCommerce services of KOBINET,
> to have a web page in six languages and e-mail address without paying any fee,
> to be guided on the preparation of their own web sites via KOBINET, i.e. web page hosting services,
> to access the information and business cooperation services of KOSGEB EIC,
> to practise on search engines and the Internet, in order to become more familiar with the technology and the world.

United States of America

There are over a thousand business service institutions established by different federal agencies and the 50 States. At the federal level, the most important programme is the Small Business Administration (SBA).

An independent agency, SBA is the most important governmental support organization focusing on SME development. SBA has a budget of almost US$ 1 billion mainly used as loans and loan guarantees, with advisory services accounting for only 10 per cent of the budget.

While SBA only gets 0.4% of the Federal budget, the taxes paid by its successful clients cover most of its budget – a clear example of cross-subsidization.

The SBA sustains a network of Small Business Development Centres (SBDCs), partnerships with the private sector, the education community and local communities, which provide local training and consulting services throughout the country. They trained over 600,000 clients in 1999 and over a million women have been trained since 1995.

An interesting business support example in the USA can be found in the National Aeronautics and Space Administration (NASA), which has an Office of Small and Disadvantaged Business Utilization (OSDBU). It exists to assist firms in obtaining contracts with NASA and sub-contracts with NASA's large contractors, and in getting involved in NASA's technology transfer.

The ODDBU is certified to evaluate its performance by using quality, quantity and institutionalization (QQI) as a measure of success. The QQI examines the extent to which NASA contracts contribute to company improvement, the amount of dollars spent, and the extent to which practices are institutionalized into permanent NASA policy.

The programmes of the Office include:
> Training on how to market to NASA, how to bid, and how to contract with NASA;
> Forums enabling SMEs to present their capabilities to NASA managers;
> Protégé programmes where big companies choose small businesses for mentor relationships;
> Advisory committee to improve relationship between the office and SMEs;
> Round Table with top 25 big businesses to improve subcontracting opportunities to small business;
> Teaching SMEs how to commercialize NASA technology.

Other forms of federal assistance to SMEs in the USA include:

> a Catalogue of Federal Domestic Assistance
> Small Business Innovation Research Program, a Government programme that taxes the largest research and development agencies and institutions and subsidizes R&D for small businesses
> the US Department of Commerce
> the Economic Development Administration
> the International Trade Administration
> the General Services Administration.

Some of these support institutions focus their services on small geographical regions and/or disadvantaged segments of the population, such as women or minorities.

PART IV
CONCLUSIONS AND RECOMMENDATIONS

CHAPTER 10.
GENERAL CONCLUSIONS

The Meeting of Experts made the following recommendations to the Governments of UNECE member States and their legislative authorities, international organizations and non-Governmental organizations (NGOs).

It was generally acknowledged that SMEs, both in advanced market economies and in transition economies, find it harder than larger businesses to find and use the information and advice they need and, thus, the Expert Meeting recognized that business advisory, counselling and information services are one of the most effective means of assisting entrepreneurs in improving the competitiveness of small businesses. Furthermore, access to shared best practices is instrumental in accelerating SME development in countries in transition and in promoting cooperation in Europe.

The participants particularly highlighted the following issues:

(a) The primary aim of business services institutions is to assist start-ups, beginners and growing SMEs and to increase their competitiveness;

(b) Diversified business services should be provided for different groups of entrepreneurs and they should be tailored to the needs of the client companies;

(c) Business Support Institutions (BSIs) should identify their goals and target groups and should be specialized in providing services;

(d) Government BSIs have to work closely with labour organizations in order to coordinate their efforts in fighting unemployment and poverty;

(e) Special advisory services and networking should be created to support women entrepreneurship in countries in transition; and

(f) Tailoring of business services to target groups and, particularly, to disadvantaged groups such as minorities and disabled persons ensures that business advisory services can reach all segments of society.

Regarding financing business services, the participants recognized that services to SMEs can be offered both free of charge and for a fee. There was a consensus among the participants that the majority of the services in countries in transition should be provided at a low cost for start-ups. However, BSIs should also create value-added services.

Subsidies are a question of "to be or not to be" for BSIs. BSIs should cover at least their operational costs but it is widely acknowledged that more subsidies are needed at the early stages. Instead of subsidizing individual entrepreneurs, subsidies should be oriented towards developing service products and activities. A voucher system was identified as a new type of subsidy. Cross-subsidization can be an advantage if local governments and other donors are willing to provide it. Cross-subsidization is very difficult to justify in the CIS countries. Sustainability, both of SMEs and of business services institutions, is a new area for consultancy and advisory services.

Business development services must be demand-driven and capable of adapting to users' needs. Competition amongst BSIs should be maintained and SMEs should be encouraged to exercise their right to select their service institution more widely. It is important to raise the awareness of the possibilities for assistance among all potential users.

The quality of business support services determines their effectiveness in the creation of successful enterprises and in the development of existing ones. The participants concluded that high-quality consultative services must be made available, too. With regard to "first-stop-shop" versus "one-stop-shop" services, the participants noted that start-ups clearly need first-stop-shops, ensuring direct contact with advisors and including several support mechanisms. To ensure better quality, support services should be linked together, using a comprehensive approach as opposed to a fragmented one.

The participants agreed that business services institutions must be monitored and evaluated. BSIs can be evaluated by examining their outreach, impact, cost efficiency, and sustainability. The clients are the best evaluators of services they receive.

There is also a clear need for structured quality assurance procedures. Evaluation criteria on the quality of BSIs has a dual character: on the one hand, there is the ISO 9000 series of standards, implementing and certifying the quality assurance system; and on the other hand, the evaluation of economic sustainability needs to be taken into account, too.

The participants noted that the business environment, including the legislative and regulatory framework, the banking system and contract enforcement, is an important condition for providing effective services to SMEs.

Governments in countries in transition should design and implement policies, specifically tailored to small business, and aimed at simplifying the business environment and, for the accession countries, converging national SME legislation with the *acquis communautaire* pertinent to small firms. Governments in transition economies should also orient their policies and programmes towards fostering entrepreneurship.

Services are most effective, when they are brought as physically close to small-scale entrepreneurs as possible. Government institutions and international organizations should use local support structures to ensure outreach to a critical mass of clients.

The use of information technology in the daily practices of SMEs must be promoted by BSIs through training and provision of technology. Web-site business dialogue could be very useful in providing information on legislative and financing issues, especially if it also provided a feedback mechanism. Both the physical proximity of business services institutions and virtual offices have their value in SME promotion. However, a virtual network should support and complement a physical network.

The creation of new products, i.e. through R&D, should be made a priority in transition economies. Transfer of technology and know-how from advanced market economies is an important part of developing an R&D capacity in transition economies.

Synergy, in the form of partnerships between Governments, legislative authorities, international organizations and BSIs, is required in the context of globalization. The best way to benefit from each experience would be for the UNECE to create an ad hoc group of experts responsible for drawing up guidelines on best practice in business advisory, counselling and information services.

CHAPTER 11.
RECOMMENDATIONS

RECOMMENDATIONS TO GOVERNMENTS AND LEGISLATIVE AUTHORITIES

Business Environment

Simplification of the business environment for SMEs is an important task of Governments. Legislative authorities are advised to create a clear and transparent legal and legislative framework for SME development.

Governments should have a policy on SME development based on creating a network of different services. Governments should prepare and implement long-term programmes for supporting SMEs that include areas such as access to financial resources, ensuring good quality and standardized services, provision of Government subsidies, training of entrepreneurs, setting up partnerships and special programmes for different target groups.

Governments should foster the sustainability of business services institutions through strong support at the initial stage; encouraging good management; employment of skilled staff; regular contacts with entrepreneurs; and provision of quality and standardized services by BSIs.

It should be a responsibility of Governments to monitor the effect of advisory services on SMEs, to remove barriers and ensure access to funds and projects that support start-ups and growing businesses.

Financial Resources

Governments should design a special financial system for the starting up and the development of SMEs, which encompasses easier access to information, business-related advice and credits, involving the banking sector, insurance companies, and other financial institutions.

Governments are in a position to concentrate financial support for SMEs by pooling international, national, local, and private resources, and by targeting groups such as start-ups, growing businesses, and innovative entrepreneurs.

Governments should create start-up funds, particularly for technology-oriented companies. At the initial stage, Governments are advised to play the main role and be a shareholder in establishing and promoting SMEs.

Human Resources, Networking and Partnerships

Governments in transition economies are encouraged to invest in human resources development and to set up special programmes for the support of business start-ups, especially among disadvantaged groups.

Governments can play a role in promoting and providing information to youth through vocational and secondary schools about the business environment, business start-ups, planning and management.

Governments can train staff working in the area of SMEs in an entrepreneurial manner, with particular emphasis on motivation.

Governments are in a position to coordinate all existing relevant Governmental and non-Governmental institutions and organizations in the SME sector as stakeholders when formulating SME policies, strategies, and programmes for SME development support.

Innovation, R&D, Intellectual Property Rights and Transfer of Technology

Governments should encourage universities and R&D institutions to collaborate with technology-oriented small and medium-sized enterprises.

Within their capabilities, Governments should encourage and support the establishment and development of innovation and technology centres, which include incubators, and they should create and develop science and technology parks.

Governments should support the creation of national network of institutions, offering information and assistance to SMEs in intellectual property rights.

Governments have a vital role to play in encouraging the application of information technology by SMEs, especially in developing web pages, e-commerce, entrepreneurial training and partner search.

RECOMMENDATIONS TO INTERNATIONAL ORGANIZATIONS

Business Environment

International organizations are asked to encourage Governments to create a business-friendly environment for entrepreneurship and SME development.

When negotiating conventions, norms and standards in economic, technical and environmental matters, international organizations should always consider the impact such activities have on each country and region and to apply a country-specific approach.

Financial Resources

Keeping in mind that business advisory services have to reach sustainability, international organizations can develop new sets of services, encouraging business services institutions (BSIs) to offer value-added services to SMEs.

Hence, international organizations are advised to help BSIs develop demand-oriented and focused services, disseminating the practice of cost recovery and cross subsidization.

International organizations can facilitate the access of countries in transition to the resources of international organizations.

Quality, Standards of Services and Monitoring

International institutions are in a position to develop and distribute among BSIs and other advisory organizations clear and operational principles of quality assurance (e.g. ISO 9,000).

The EIC Network and other networks of the European Commission can be used for monitoring several activities in the countries of their location, especially in accession countries.

Human Resources, Networking and Partnerships

International organizations can help Governments of member countries to prepare strategies and long-term programmes for SME development.

They can assist in establishing business support centres, incubators, and other business services institutions and can help them to create proper services for SMEs.

International organizations should keep in mind the principles of subsidiarity and networking, and bring services as close as possible to SMEs.

Given the difficulty for local BSIs to develop a full range of services for SMEs, partnerships are to be encouraged and facilitated by international organizations.

International organizations can act as good intermediaries between advanced market and transition economies in helping the latter with data collection, information on good practices in the business service development, and the preparation of action plans on how to implement best practices in transition economies.

RECOMMENDATIONS TO NON-GOVERNMENTAL ORGANIZATIONS

NGOs can contribute to simplifying and improving the administrative and legislative environment for SMEs by lobbying Governments, providing information, marketing, and advocacy work.

NGOs can improve SME access to finances by assisting in the search for partners at the local, national and international levels.

Often providers of training, technical and legal assistance, NGOs help SMEs to internationalize their strategies by providing them with information and other standardized services.

They are in a position to boost the competitiveness of SMEs and introduce them to research, innovation, and standards through their own networks, mechanisms for exchanging best practice, and access to information technology.

NGOs can foster the spirit of entrepreneurship by encouraging individuals to become entrepreneurs. They should continue to support target groups such as young people, women, and disabled persons through special programmes.

NGOs can play a vital role in a continuing dialogue between public and private entities responsible for entrepreneurial activities.